The Rise of the Insane State – What is Happening to the U.S. Economy?

Kenneth R. Szulczyk

The Rise of the Insane State – What is Happening to the U.S. Economy?

Cover design by Kenneth R. Szulczyk

Published by KDP, ISBN: 978-1709580888

Edition 6.0, July 2024

Table of Contents

Forward

This book examines self-interest. Politicians, attorneys, bureaucrats, business people, and people do not look at government and think about how to improve our laws, rules, and regulations. Instead, they analyze our legal system, devising and scheming how to benefit personally from the legal system.

Under a capitalistic system, profits drive self-interest. Thus, a person can use this simple rule to predict outcomes. A person asks one question - how does one profit from this situation? On the other hand, government and public institutions rarely follow a profit motive. Whims, notions, beliefs, and prejudices guide their self-interest and constantly change. If the government evolves into a large controlling institution, it opens the doors to an insane asylum. Unfortunately, those doors flung violently open in the 1990s in the United States as Americans witnessed the death of common sense. Hence, we arrive at the title of this book, "The Rise of the Insane State."

The ideas in this book are universal. As I travel more, I identify the same struggle between the government and its people, which I find pretty eerie. Although the names and places change, all governments behave similarly, as all government officials control and dominate their people.

1. The Purpose of Government

"In this present crisis, government is not the solution to our problem, government is the problem..."

-Ronald Reagan

Since the dawn of civilization, humans have gazed upward into the stars and heavens to search for the almighty God. God embodies the all-powerful being who was the grand architect of the universe and created all life on Earth. From the heavens, God watches over his creation. Then men and women kneel down before God and whisper prayers. People believe God is listening and that God will intervene in their lives and answer their prayers with miracles.

Another powerful entity exists in society and lies at the heart of our civilization. This entity has evolved into the second most influential force in nature. This is familiar to us because that entity is the government. A government has immense power over its people. A government can imprison or execute its citizens, confiscate property, or send its army and navy to invade another country. A government intervenes in the daily lives of its citizens. It imposes laws, rules, and regulations over everyone under its domain while it collects taxes from its citizens. No other entity in our society has that power.

People place too much faith in their government. They ask government officials and politicians to save them, make our society better off, or correct an injustice. Unfortunately, our political leaders and government officials comply happily. Now, all levels of government in the United States meddle in all society's affairs. Our government shackled all our businesses, industries, and markets with numerous and confusing laws, regulations, and taxes.

The U.S. economy remains stuck and mired in a perpetual recession. The unemployment rate remains frozen at nearly 10%, and experts predicted a new recession in 2012. Many Americans believe capitalism has failed. Our political leaders remain in a state of denial as they keep fueling the size of our government. They refuse to reduce government spending in line with revenues or reign in their crazy rules and regulations. They believe the government must step in to stop the economic decline.

The government cannot be a savior, and a government solution can never work. Only the American people can lift themselves out of this perpetual depression. However, Americans first need to remove the shackles of government control.

One premise we will get from this book is that it is a terrible idea to keep expanding government. The government can do great things, but it can also blunder badly. Although a society needs a government, a large government creates many more problems than it solves. Instead, the government should encourage people to be entrepreneurs and work hard to lift themselves up. People should not depend on the government for their livelihood and salvation.

We have an easy solution to our perpetual recession, and it entails two parts. First, the government's size should be kept as small as possible with limited power. An expanding government always creates more problems than it solves. Each chapter in this book hones this simple fact. Second, religion is a critical component of society. Religions impose constraints on human behavior. They become a source of values, morals, and ethics. Furthermore, many religions espouse hard work and family values. If 99% of the population followed a good religion, then society functions by itself without the guiding hand of government. People with strong pious values do not need government watching over them and meddling in their affairs. Thus, society runs itself.

The Government Creates the Legal System

Every society needs a government. The government establishes a legal system that glues society together. It influences how people work, save, and consume, as well as the level of freedom that people and businesses enjoy. The United States became the world's richest country because the Founding Fathers instituted an excellent legal structure that encouraged Americans to be independent, hard-working entrepreneurs. Our legal system allowed them to keep their fruits of labor. Consequently, free enterprise created America's immense wealth as the government stood on the sideline and let its citizens create and garner wealth.

A legal system is difficult to define. The best way to describe it is by comparing it to its opposite – chaos. Chaos prevents a society or an economy from forming. As people organize themselves, a legal system evolves that defines its citizens' rules, rights, and expectations. Some entities elevate themselves above their citizens, becoming the enforcers and protectors of these rules, rights, and expectations. This enforcer and protector become the government. The government establishes the legal system and the "rules of the game."

A government can create an excellent legal system. A sound legal system helps citizens settle disputes, protects private property, and encourages citizens to interact harmoniously and peacefully. Furthermore, an excellent legal system encourages the growth and expansion of businesses. Thus, private enterprise increases a society's wealth. On the other hand, a flawed legal system divides people, encourages animosity and hatred between groups, and creates overly complicated rules and laws. Hence, a flawed legal system chokes and suffocates businesses, eventually annihilating society's wealth.

A legal system comprises society's rules, practices, laws, regulations, customs, and habits. It always imposes limits and boundaries on human behavior but simultaneously allows citizens to react together in predictable ways [1]. For example, zoning laws impose limits on residential neighborhoods. One neighbor cannot build a factory in the center of a residential neighborhood. Hence, the residents of the neighborhood benefit. They do not worry about a factory's pollution, noise, and traffic. When a new person moves into the neighborhood, they expect no one will build a factory there. Although a legal system limits human behavior, an excellent legal system allows people to predict behavior and make future decisions.

Governments constantly change and tinker with the laws, rules, and regulations. When the government changes the legal system, the change always creates winners and losers. Some citizens benefit, while the government penalizes the other citizens. For example, the government imposes a speed limit on drivers of cars and trucks. To the speeders, this law imposes a limit on their behavior. However, the roads become safer for other drivers and pedestrians as everyone drives at a safer speed. The trick is to change the law so more people benefit than are penalized. Therefore, a society grows and thrives if a government changes the rules and regulations prudently.

An excellent legal system requires equality, order, predictability, and stability.

> **Equality:** Laws apply to everyone equally. If the government granted a group preferential treatment, then the disadvantaged groups would view their government as capricious and corrupt. Furthermore, they could become bitter, lose faith in the legal system, and become criminals or violators. For example, if judges always ruled in favor of women for cases involving women versus men, then men would harbor acrid feelings against women and the court system. Current domestic violence and sexual harassment laws are dividing men and women in the United States. Equality has one requirement – laws apply equally to the political leaders in government. Many members of Congress forget about this as they pass new laws exempting themselves [1].

> **Order:** The legal system establishes order. Laws inform people how to interact with each other. Laws should be simple, clear, and understandable. Everyone with a shred of common sense can comply with them. Furthermore, the government should keep the number of laws to a minimum. For example, the Ten Commandants are straightforward and concise. "Thou shall not steal" encompasses a wide variety of crimes. Stealing is stealing. It makes no difference whether a person steals someone's car or a person's identity to obtain credit. Unfortunately, U.S. laws have become so complicated that the experts have trouble understanding them. If the experts cannot understand the rules, how can Americans without legal training understand them?

> **Predictability:** Laws create predictability. People can predict relationships and reduce their uncertainty when they

know the laws and regulations. For example, if we agree to buy land, we exchange cash for the deed. What would happen if we purchased the land, where we exchanged cash for the deed, but the government did not transfer the title to our name? This example seems foolish, but this happens in Northern Mexico. Poorly defined property rights would hamper economic growth and development.

> **Stability:** The legal system must be stable. For example, the government changed all the laws and regulations one morning after we awakened. How would we know if we comply with the new laws and regulations? Again, this example seems foolish, but the U.S. federal and state governments continually change the laws, rules, and regulations. Stability does not mean rules become rigid and fixed. As society changes, the rules and regulations for the legal system must keep pace with societal changes [2].

These laws are efficient if they create equality, order, predictability, and stability. Examples of efficient laws include the following:

> **Example 1:** A law forces everyone to drive on the same side of the road. Someone driving on the opposite side of the road could cause an accident, endangering the public.

> **Example 2:** Laws protect people's private property. People work hard so they can buy things with their salary. If a thief can steal a person's stuff without legal consequences, people have little incentive to work. Hard-working people would stop working and become thieves. Unfortunately, professionals within the U.S. legal system have become good at stealing legally from people.

> **Example 3:** Laws punish drunk drivers because alcohol impairs a person's ability to operate machinery properly.

Thus, a drunk driver could injure, maim, or kill innocent bystanders while driving intoxicated.

Humans are opportunistic. Some must violate society's rules, with the most severe violations being rape and murder. Therefore, a legal system must impose sanctions and punish violators [2]. Punishment informs people about the rules and regulations and encourages citizens to comply with the laws.

All legal systems have severe flaws. They use a legal language that describes the circumstances and transactions of its citizens. As circumstances and society become more complicated, the legal language becomes more complex, giving birth to new, more complicated rules, laws, and regulations [2]. Over time, a more complex legal system requires more bureaucrats and better-educated bureaucrats. Then government bureaucrats evolve into a dominant class in society. They can artificially expand their power and salaries by extending the rules and regulations or creating an overly complicated legal structure. This rising class of bureaucrats could aid the growth and intrusiveness of government, creating many problems for society. Therefore, bureaucrats pursuing their self-interest can work against the economy, destroying people's incentive to build wealth.

Economic Systems

Experts in economics and political science define two types of legal systems: socialism and capitalism. A socialistic government owns and controls all society's property, land, buildings, and machines. Socialistic governments do not use markets to direct economic activity. Instead, a central government committee determines production levels and prices, which they conveniently call "collective decision making." (They always think about the people). Then the state produces and distributes all goods and services to its citizens.

An extreme form of socialism is communism. Karl Marx believed society would evolve into its highest form without social classes or class struggles. However, the government must control all aspects of its citizens' lives and help transition towards this utopia. The Soviet Union represents the premier example of communism. The Soviet state produced all consumer goods and services for 70 years. Soviet people could buy two types of T.V. sets: color and black and white, about five types of soda, several types of bread, and three car models: Lada, Moskvich, and Volga. Several Soviet products were okay, while others had quality issues. For example, the color T.V. set could explode while the Moskvich was a junky car.

Many Soviet products were also in short supply, so not all citizens could buy and own cars. The Soviet system had a pecking order: Communist party members came first, academe and scientists were second, and everyone else was last, although communism was supposed to erase social classes and make everyone equal.

The Soviet system pushed Russia into becoming a world power during the 20th century. Nevertheless, it came at a significant cost. During the 1980s, the Soviet economy stagnated, causing severe shortages. Consumers shopped in their stores with bare shelves. However, the Soviet Union had a pecking order; communist party members shopped in their stores filled with products and merchandise. Finally, the Soviet Union maintained an extensive prison system, the Gulag, that the state filled with prisoners while Stalin executed millions of Soviet citizens through his purges.

Communism is still around. North Korea uses communism, while. the communists still control China and Cuba, even though the leaders incorporate markets and private property into their societies, i.e., communism does not generate wealth.

Socialism has a problem - the government wants everyone to be equal. The famous socialistic quote is, "From each according to his means, to each according to his needs." Unfortunately, this represents the antithesis of humankind's nature. Humans possess different talents, work ethics, and values. This inequality in human abilities always causes socialism to fail. For example, suppose a hard-working farmer produces 100 bushels of apples while a lazy one produces 20 bushels. In that case, a socialistic government will take 40 bushels of apples away from the hard-working farmer and give it to the lazy one. Thus, each has 60 bushels of apples, and they become equal.

Socialism discourages hard work. For example, the hard-working farmer will start producing 20 bushels of apples, preventing the government's seizure of his apples and, indirectly, his hard work. Of course, the government bureaucrat will not give all 40 apples to the poor farmer. Bureaucrats must eat, too, feeding off the hard-working and diligent. Unfortunately, socialism tends to reduce everyone to the lowest common denominator. The slowest, laziest people set the standards in society.

Under a capitalistic system, a hard-working farmer could sell his excess supply of apples to the market, earning a profit. Hence, the farmer receives a reward for his hard work. Consequently, capitalism, hard work, and self-interest work together, creating a solid backbone for an economy.

Laissez-faire capitalism is the opposite of communism. Laissez faire means let it be. People own all property, land, buildings, and machines, producing and distributing goods and services to other citizens. Capitalism is synonymous with free markets because citizens use markets to freely transfer resources, goods, services, and property with little government interference. Nevertheless, capitalism still needs a government! The government establishes the legal system or the "rules of the game."

The United States was a capitalistic country during the 19th century, and we became a world power at the beginning of the 20th century with a high standard of living. However, we lost our way. Federal, state, and local governments extensively use taxes, subsidies, price controls, and regulations to control our economy. For example, Americans can still own property in title only. If a homeowner builds a house, do they own that house? Governments at all levels impose many conditions on homeowners. They must apply for permits, adhere to building and zoning codes, and pay property taxes.

Some states have high property taxes, and the municipal government quickly forecloses on a homeowner's property for not paying them. Moreover, homeowners need permission from the government to alter or change their property. If a homeowner builds on a wetland or endangers a species going extinct, then they can get into serious trouble with the U.S. government. Except for property taxes, we survived the 19th century without all these rules and regulations as we constructed our massive cities.

Federal, state, and local governments have violated private property rights for 40 years. As we progress toward the 21st century, our society has become more socialistic and highly regulated. Are we better off, or has our society started crumbling?

China was a communist country, and the government-owned all the property. Since the 1970s, the Chinese government gradually opened their society to free markets, competition, and private property ownership. They use free markets and capitalism to build their wealth and create jobs. Their manufacturing industries are booming as they transformed extensive marshes into cities overnight. As Americans shop at a store, they are likely to buy a product produced by a Chinese corporation. Consequently, capitalism revived the Chinese dragon, and it continues propelling China into a world power. After the 2008 Financial Crisis, China grew furiously and intensely while the United States and Europe continued sinking.

Capitalism is not a perfect system. However, it is the best system that we have at our disposal. The only alternative to capitalism is a form of government control. Unfortunately, the government cannot create wealth. Otherwise, the Soviet Union would have grown into the wealthiest country in the world, and it would not have collapsed in 1991. Everyone heard the stories of Soviet people standing in lines for hours to receive their bread ration or how the Soviet state industries produced low-quality goods. Furthermore, the Chinese government moved away from communism because it failed and unleashed the power of capitalism and free markets. Thus, the government cannot create wealth; only citizens and businesses through private markets can create wealth.

Rapidly Expanding Government

The United States has two political parties: The Republicans and the Democrats. The Democrats believe in equality, the opportunity to go to college, support a clean environment, and universal healthcare. Thus, the Democrats espouse a growing, expanding government because they support social programs that help the disadvantaged. On the other hand, the Republicans espouse a capitalistic system. In theory, they believe in a small, limited government with low tax rates, favorable regulations on business, and a strong national defense. The Republicans should contract the government and limit its size. However, both political parties expand the government, regardless of political philosophy.

Political parties strive for control over the government. Then they use the government to strengthen their political agendas and further their self-interest. For example, George W. Bush, a Republican and the 43rd President of the United States, expanded the government during his two terms in office, even though he claimed he supported limited government. He founded the new Department of Homeland Security, entered into wars with Afghanistan and Iraq, and passed numerous controversial laws. One law, the No Child Left Behind Act, allows the federal government to interfere with local school systems. President Bush also signed into law Medicare Part D. The Federal government provides prescription drug insurance for seniors as a way for politicians to buy votes from senior citizens. Finally, President Bush nationalized corporations and banks that teetered on bankruptcy during the 2008 Financial Crisis. He transferred approximately $700 billion in taxpayer money to bail out the financial system, although many Americans opposed it. His predecessor, President Clinton, a Democrat, slowed the government's growth and generated budget surpluses during his last term in office.

The Republicans at the state and local levels of government are just as bad as the U.S. Presidents. For example, Governor Rick Perry, a Republican, started the franchise tax in Texas. He invented an income tax on businesses without calling it an income tax. The tax circumvents the voter's right to vote and pass an income tax in Texas. Governor Mitt Romney, another Republican, passed a universal healthcare program in Massachusetts, which President Obama used to establish his new federal healthcare program.

Bureaucrats, politicians, and leaders are increasing government size, scope, and mission. The U.S. federal, state, and local governments are passing laws at a furious rate that they have detonated a legal atomic bomb. More laws, rules, and regulations require more bureaucrats. Thus, the government continually expands or creates new bureaucracies.

The government must pay for its army of bureaucrats and has three funding sources:

> ➤ The government could collect taxes, fees, and fines. However, excessively high taxes, fees, and penalties can stifle a market economy, depressing incomes and wealth. Unfortunately, the public does not like taxes. Thus, politicians and bureaucrats resorted to numerous small taxes, fees, and fines, causing a painful death from a million paper cuts.

> ➤ The government could borrow money. Borrowing money creates future tax liabilities because the government must repay the money plus interest. When governments borrow money, they hope the economy grows, expanding the tax base. Then the government repays the debt by collecting more significant future tax revenue. This strategy could be disastrous if an economy begins contracting and stagnating. Some people believe the United States will enter an extended two-decade recession similar to Japan's.

> ➤ The government can print money. This option is only available to the federal government through our central bank, the Federal Reserve System. However, printing money is a terrible option because it leads to inflation. As prices rise, wage increases usually lag behind price increases, squeezing the workers, which economists call the inflation tax. Furthermore, a high inflation rate weakens and depreciates a currency. Some people believe a massive U.S. government debt will lead to high inflation and the collapse of the U.S.

dollar. Then hard economic times will begin. The 2007 Great Recession will pale in comparison.

Most politicians across the world today use Keynesian economics. They use deficit spending, which always leads to the accumulation of debt. Politicians increase spending or decrease taxes, which expands the economy and causes a budget deficit. They use deficit spending during recessions and booms. Unfortunately, a growing government debt becomes a potential ticking time bomb. Once investors lose faith in the government to repay its debt, the government experiences a crisis. The government must raise taxes or contract government spending, hindering economic growth and creating a period of stagnation. If politicians used Keynesian economics correctly, a government should have budget surpluses during a boom cycle and deficits during recessions. The boom cycle allows the government to pay down its debt during good times.

The U.S. federal government cannot restrain its spending and has operated large budget deficits since the 1960s. Before the 1960s, politicians only accumulated debt when we were at war. During times of peace, politicians would repay the public debt. During the 1960s, President Johnson started the War on Poverty and escalated the Vietnam War. Then President Nixon began the War on Drugs.

Since then, perpetual budget deficits have plagued the United States as our public debt continually rises. Figure 1 shows the U.S. federal debt starting with the 1950s, surpassing the $14.5 trillion mark in 2011. U.S. debt will attain new heights with President Obama's $787 billion economic stimulus package and President Bush's $700 billion Wall Street bailout package in October 2008. Unfortunately, the public debt grew at 7.5% annually for the last 60 years, surpassing our 3% economic growth rate.

As of March 2012, the U.S. government held about $4.8 trillion, or approximately 32% of the U.S. debt. Social Security Administration and federal retirement accounts invest their funds and budget surpluses in U.S. government securities.

Although Social Security had surpluses for the last 20 years, Congress already spent this money and replaced it with U.S. Treasury Securities [3]. This is equivalent to putting money in a cookie jar. Then we decide to spend the money and replace the money with IOUs. This trick only works if we do not dig ourselves into a large financial pit. After reaching a point, the government can no longer refund Social Security with its money. In 2011, the Social Security fund had a $45 billion deficit, and Congress can no longer treat Social Security as free money, which is one reason why the U.S. government deficits have persistently exceeded a trillion dollars every year since 2008. This situation is unsustainable and will have negative consequences.

Figure 1: U.S. Government Debt

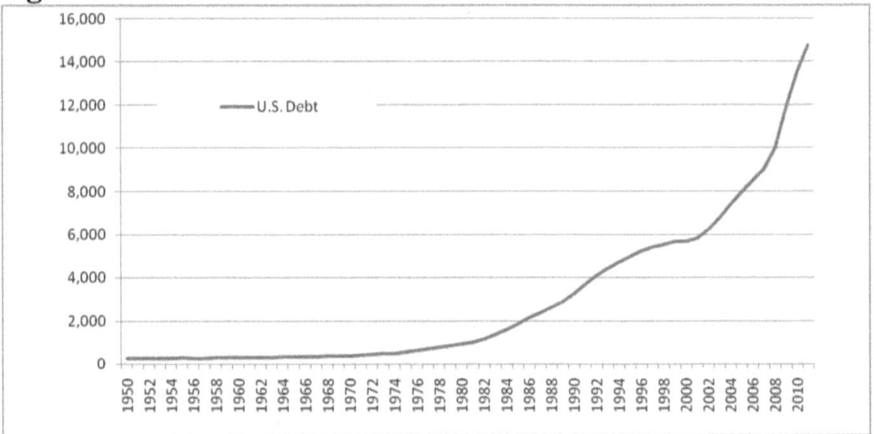

The Federal Reserve System held about $1.7 trillion or approximately 11% as of March 2012 [3]. The Federal Reserve maintains the nation's money supply and buys U.S. Government Securities to expand it. The 2007 Great Recession was severe, and the U.S. economy struggled. Consequently, the Federal Reserve granted banks $2 trillion in emergency loans, keeping the U.S. financial system afloat. The chairman, Ben Bernanke, euphemistically calls this quantitative easing. The Federal Reserve purchased toxic mortgages from banks, granted loans to the European Central Bank, and bought truckloads of U.S. government securities. Unfortunately, the inflation rate will spike if the banks begin lending to the public, injecting these funds into the economy.

Massive debt is only part of the story. A growing economy expands the government's tax base, enabling the government to finance more debt. Furthermore, a flourishing economy requires more infrastructure and bureaucrats, such as roads, highways, schools, and government services.

Economists use Gross Domestic Product (GDP) to measure the economy's size. A growing GDP indicates our society produces more goods and services while incomes rise. Figure 2 shows the federal government debt relative to the GDP. During the 1950s, government debt quickly dropped as the government repaid its war debts. Before the 1970's, the U.S. government only accumulated debt to finance wars. Since the 1980s, government debt has taken off from President Reagan's massive government deficits, and the debt-GDP ratio currently exceeds 100%. Usually, investors stop buying debt when it becomes too high. For example, the investors stopped buying the Greek government's debt when the debt-GDP ratio reached 140%.

Figure 2: U.S. Federal Government Debt relative to GDP

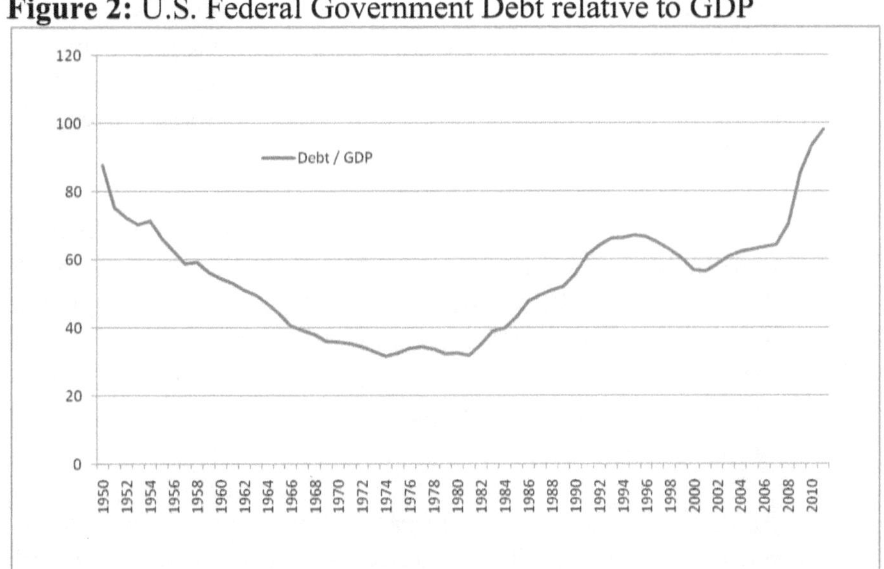

Government debt can positively affect the economy if the government invests in infrastructure, education, or research. Then public spending benefits both the current and future generations. Future citizens benefit from more knowledge, highways, libraries, and universities. For example, the U.S. government funds research institutions such as the National Aeronautics and Space Administration (NASA). In turn, NASA buys billions of dollars in parts from hi-tech industries. These hi-tech industries hire more scientists and engineers and expand their research and development. Thus, white-collar jobs flourish in our economy.

Society benefits if a government spends and invests its money wisely. However, a large government debt has five potential problems.

> **Problem 1:** Future generations are saddled with repaying this debt. Suppose the government wastes money on unwinnable wars, incarcerates people for minor crimes, or bails out corporations that make terrible financial decisions. In that case, the government wastes this money, and future generations receive no benefits. For example, the U.S. government poured billions of dollars into the War on Poverty and the War on Drugs. We lost both wars, but our government continues fighting these wars. The U.S. government also started the decade-long wars in Afghanistan and Iraq.

> **Problem 2:** A large government debt crowds out private investment. When an investor buys a U.S. Treasury bond, they are unable to use the same money to invest in private businesses. This scenario is a direct result of a large, expanding government that heavily borrows, which in turn, hampers private investment and leads to economic stagnation.

> **Problem 3:** As the debt increases, the government must pay more interest. In 2011, interest on the debt was the fifth largest item in the federal budget. When interest on the debt becomes the largest item in the budget, government debt

becomes out of control, and Congress will cut funding to other governmental programs.

➢ **Problem 4:** A growing debt indicates an expanding government. A large government debt expands the government's size, scope, and mission.

➢ **Problem 5:** A large government debt can trigger a financial crisis. Some of the debt becomes due daily, and the government rolls over the expiring debt by issuing new debt. If investors lose faith in the government's ability to repay the debt, they stop buying the debt, triggering a crisis. This can lead to a situation where the central bank must buy the government debt, which in turn can spark high inflation, further exacerbating the crisis.

The Optimal Size of Government

The U.S. federal government's budget mushroomed to $3.8 trillion, or nearly 25.3% of the U.S. economy in 2011. Table 1 shows the major items in the budget and includes on-budget and off-budget items. The government defines Social Security and the U.S. Postal Office as off-budget. The most significant expenditures include national defense, social security, income security, and Medicare. Income security is the safety net programs, such as housing assistance, food stamps, etc. Finally, the government paid the debt of $207 billion in net interest.

Is our government's size hindering our economic growth? The Rahn Curve illustrates the relationship between the size of the government and a country's economic growth rate. Richard Rahn estimated the optimal level of government spending lay between 15 and 25% of GDP. If a government spends beyond 25% of GDP, then it hinders economic growth. Currently, the U.S. government spends approximately 25.3%, which represents one piece of our government. After we add state and local governments, the government spending lies between 35 and 40% of GDP. Similarly, the United Kingdom is about 43% of GDP while many European countries exceed 50%. After the 2007 Great Recession, these countries experienced terrible economic growth rates. On the other hand, the Asian Tigers - Hong Kong, Singapore, South Korea, and Taiwan have government spending within the optimal range, and their economies are flourishing.

Table 1: The 2011 U.S. Government Budget

Budget Item	Amount ($ millions)
National Defense	768,217
Social Security	748,354
Income Security	622,654
Medicaid	494,343
Net Interest on the Debt	206,688
Total Budget	**3,818,819**

Source: U.S. Printing Office. Budget of the United States Government.
   Available at http://www.gpo.gov/ (Accessed on 3/24/12)

The Rahn Curve has a weakness. It classifies all government spending as equal. If a government provides generous social and retirement programs, these programs do not boost GDP growth rates. However, if the government invests in education, training, or infrastructure, these investments can boost future GDP growth rates. As Table 1 shows, the four largest items in the U.S. budget include the military, retirement, and social programs. Unfortunately, the U.S. government is not investing in the U.S. economy.

The Rahn Curve places a lower bound on the government's size. Economists experience difficulties measuring our government's size, scope, and mission. Federal, state, and local governments established various quasi-government agencies, authorities, nonprofit organizations, and public corporations. Some refer to this as hidden government because these institutions have little government oversight, are not liable to the voters, and can issue debt through the government's name. Some institutions became riddled with corruption, mismanagement, bid rigging, or maintaining the "good ole boy system" [4].

Several examples of hidden government include:

- ➢ Local and state governments founded organizations to operate airports, seaports, toll bridges, low-income housing, parks, schools, and universities [4]. If these institutions experience financial problems, the local or state government could be liable for their debt.

- ➢ Some city governments established public corporations or departments to provide utilities for their residents, such as water, electricity, or natural gas. Then the public corporations and departments charge high prices and funnel some of the profits to the local government.

- ➢ The federal government created public corporations such as the Federal National Mortgage Association (Fannie Mae), the Federal Home Loan Mortgage Corporation (Freddie Mac), and the Student Loan Marketing Association (Sallie Mae). Fannie Mae and Freddie Mac grant mortgages to low-income households, while Sallie Mae grants loans to college students.

Governments established these institutions to benefit their citizens. However, these institutions do not act like private businesses. The purpose of a personal business is to earn profits. If an owner mismanages a private business, provides low-quality products, or offers terrible customer service, then that business could fail and become bankrupt. The threat of financial failure forces a business to pay attention to the market, its customers, and its products and services, or the business fails. Unfortunately, fiscal failure provides little feedback to public institutions. Public institutions can run to the government and beg for subsidies, tax breaks, or favors to keep inefficient, mismanaged public corporations operating.

Public corporations can experience a large financial exposure to changes in a market, generating losses in the billions. For example, the housing market bubble popped in 2007, causing housing prices to tumble. Moreover, the 2007 Great Recession caused soaring unemployment and foreclosure rates. Banks lose money when families stop paying their mortgages as they foreclose on homes. Then banks pay legal fees and court costs to take possession of a house that has lost market value. Unfortunately, Fannie Mae and Freddie Mac hold roughly half the mortgages in the United States, which equaled about $12 trillion. The U.S. government has already spent billions of dollars to bail out these two financial institutions [5]. As of January 2010, Fannie Mae and Freddie Mac accumulated $400 billion in losses [6], which equaled $1,333 for every man, woman, and child in the United States.

Sallie Mae and the student-loan market could also experience financial exposure to changes in the market. The 2007 Great Recession was the worst recession since the Great Depression. Although the recession ended in 2009, the U.S. economy failed to create jobs for college graduates. These college graduates will default on their debt if they cannot find jobs. The default rate hovered around 24% in 2012. For example, a college graduate enters the workforce with an average student-loan debt of $24,000, while law school graduates and other professional graduates accumulate student-loan balances exceeding $100,000. Consequently, the federal government could pay billions to cover its student loan guarantees to bail out Sallie Mae if it goes under.

Conclusion

The book's premise is the political system does not make a difference. For instance, communism in Russia did not fail because of communism; it failed because the government tried to control its entire economy. A democracy trying to control its entire economy will meet the same disastrous failure. The critical issue is whether private individuals or businesses make decisions or whether the government must control everything. With people and companies, they have simple goals: to better themselves or earn profits. A government can have convoluted, vague, and constantly changing goals. The reader shall discover that politicians and bureaucrats have self-interest and want to better themselves but at the expense of everyone else. Thus, what matters is how the government defines its relationships with government institutions, businesses, and people matters. A country's legal system defines these relationships.

This book emphasizes the takeover of the U.S. economy by an ever-expanding government and its bureaucrats. An expanding government is creeping socialism but not the traditional socialism where government devises a plan to build a better society or provide benefits to its citizens, such as free healthcare or free college education. Instead, the United States is evolving to a virulent form of socialism that allows individuals and businesses to own property, but bureaucrats control and monitor the use of the property with intrusive government oversight. This rising class of bureaucrats believes they have the right to interfere in all society's affairs, from family matters to personal business decisions. No issue is too small or private to elicit the bureaucrats' scrutiny. Bureaucrats in government today interfere actively in families, businesses, and all private matters.

References

[1] Dobel. J. Patrick. 1978. "The Corruption of a State." *The American Political Science Review* 72(3): 958-973

[2] Bromley, Daniel W. 1989. *Economic Interests and Institutions: The Conceptual foundations of Public Policy*. New York: Basil Blackwell. Chapter 3, "The Nature of Institutions"

[3] Treasury Bulletin. March 2012. "Ownership of Federal Securities." Available at http://www.fms.treas.gov/bulletin/index.html (03/25/12).

[4] Searcey, Dionne. July 19, 2004. "Hidden government." *Newsday.com*

[5] Goodman, Peter S. July 14, 2008. "Government as the Big Lender." *The New York Times*.

[6] Liu, Betty and Matthew Leising. December 31, 2009. "U.S. to Lose $400 Billion on Fannie, Freddie, Wallison Says." *Business Week*. Available at http://www.businessweek.com/news/2009-12-31/u-s-to-lose-400-billion-on-fannie-freddie-wallison-says.html?source=patrick.net (access date 01/04/2010).

2. Crazy Laws

"The marvel of all history is the patience with which men and women submit to burdens unnecessarily laid upon them by their governments."

-William Edgar Borah

When the Founding Fathers created the United States, being a member of Congress was a part-time job. Congressmen held jobs outside of government, usually farmers or businessmen. This differs sharply from our contemporary Congressmen because a part-time legislature provides three benefits.

> ➢ **Benefit 1:** The Founding Fathers had the insight of owning and running a business or farm. Politicians remained in touch with the people and passed laws that sustained a strong private business climate.

> ➢ **Benefit 2:** The Founding Fathers had little time to analyze and pass laws because they worked part-time. Politicians would focus on critical business rather than wasting it on frivolous matters.

> ➢ **Benefit 3:** The Founding Fathers were not career politicians. Career politicians earn their income from their government jobs. If they lose an election, then they become unemployed. A career politician may show little authentic leadership and always cater to special interest groups. Thus, career politicians do not want to offend anyone because they do not want to lose an election.

Currently, many Congressmen are lawyers and do not manage a farm or business. They lost touch with the working people and the meaning of capitalism. Furthermore, Congressmen work full-time as they employ an army of staff. Consequently, their job is to keep passing laws and regulations.

Legislators are not concerned with whether the law is good or bad or, more importantly, the long-term consequences of new laws.

They see a heart-wrenching story on the news and instantly pass a new law without regard to logic or long-term consequences, even if the law achieves the opposite effect. Congressmen and state legislators rarely appeal these laws. They keep busy passing new laws.

Legislators must pass laws so they can provide feedback to their constituents that they are working. They pass new laws at a furious rate and write them in confusing and vague language. Due to many confusing and contradictory laws, the current U.S. legal system has become disorganized and illogical.

Thoughtless legislators passed the following laws:

> **Example 1:** The city council in Chico, California, passed two pages of ordinances for using nuclear weapons within city limits. The law states, "No person shall produce, test, maintain, or store within the city a nuclear weapon..." The city attorney will file charges with the appropriate court for violations of this law [1]. However, this is a national security issue and domain of the federal government. If someone detonated a nuclear weapon within city limits, the city would no longer be there.

> **Example 2:** The city council in Pacific Grove, California, passed an ordinance that makes it a crime for a person to molest or interfere with monarch butterflies [2]. A violation is a $500 fine.

> **Example 3:** Los Angeles County passed a law that allows taco truck vendors to park their trucks for an hour. Once the hour is over, they must move to a new location. A judge could fine violators up to $1,000 or sentence them up to six months in jail. The law aims to help local restaurants because restaurant owners believe taco truck drivers have a cost advantage [3]. However, Los Angeles has air pollution problems, and enforcing this law will not help lower pollution levels.

Governments passed these crazy laws, so someone must enforce them. Does the City of Chico employ enforcement officers with Geiger counters running around the city searching for nuclear weapons violations? Does the City of Pacific Grove have officers monitoring the butterflies and ensuring people are not molesting the butterflies? Do police or inspectors in Los Angeles follow taco drivers around and ensure they park for less than an hour? Do governments have so much resources and time that they can dedicate officers to enforce these crazy laws?

Legislators and Congressmen need to understand the laws can create the opposite behavior. For example, the public and politicians became disgusted by rap and rock music's profanity and explicit language. Under threat from the federal government to pass a new law and give the Federal Trade Commission vast new authority [4], the music companies decided to self-regulate and place advisory labels on CDs and audiocassette tapes. No one under the age of 18 can buy music with explicit language.

The actual outcome of this self-regulation was the exact opposite. Labels drew attention to the language contained in music. Thus, young people, being naturally rebellious, listen to profanity-laced lyrics. Furthermore, minors can find adults who will buy this music for them. Consequently, several rappers competed for the most advisory labels on their music as these advisory labels became status symbols to musicians and rebellious teenagers.

Congress and the President passed another bad law—the Digital Millennium Copyright Act (DMCA). They wanted to protect artists and authors from online piracy while enhancing copyright laws. Piracy on the internet continues flourishing as some people download pirated books, music, movies, and software. Artists, authors, and software creators should be awarded for their creations, and people should not be allowed to enjoy copyrighted material freely.

The law has two parts. First, defeating or circumventing any encryption system used in "electronic" media is unlawful. Second, designing, distributing, or selling technologies that allow circumvention is illegal.

Law has the following six impacts:

➢ **Impact 1:** A person cannot buy a CD or DVD and make a copy. For example, what happens if a person wants to listen to his CD on an MP3 player or watch his DVD on his iPhone? This involves decrypting the media and changing its format. The federal government says this is legal, or at least has not made it illegal yet. Regulators change their interpretation of laws over time, especially if they need to boost their arrest numbers.

➢ **Impact 2:** In 2001, Russian programmer Dmitry Sklyarov was arrested in the United States for violating the DMCA. Although he did not illegally distribute copyrighted material, he wrote a program that could convert Adobe's Advanced e-Book Processor to Adobe PDF files. The conversion eliminated the safety measures embedded in the e-Book Processor. Dmitry's arrest stirred up fear among computer programmers. Consequently, foreign computer programmers avoid the United States and hold computer conferences outside the United States to escape this bad law.

➢ **Impact 3:** A student wrote a program called Embed that allows fonts to be embedded into a document. That way, computer users do not worry about a program switching fonts when they use their files on another computer. Although the student used his program for his fonts, he was sued because the program also works for copyrighted fonts. Thus, this law could hinder innovation.

➢ **Impact 4:** Sony sued competitors who wrote emulator programs for computers. An emulator allows people to play Sony Playstation Games on PCs. The Playstation, X-Box, and Nintendo are computers. All games could be played on one computer system. Unfortunately, these companies want us to buy their console that enhances their profits. Moreover, a company can sue a competitor by claiming the competitor reverse-engineered its product, thus violating this law.

Consequently, this law reduces competition and protects large companies.

- ➢ **Impact 5:** Anyone can threaten a website's administrator to remove objectionable material, inciting a violation of the DMCA. Administrators routinely comply because they are afraid to violate this law. Google lists the number of DMCA complaints when users do searches because some search results are removed. Hence, companies use this law to restrict free speech.

- ➢ **Impact 6:** This law only applies to the United States. However, the internet is worldwide. People in the United States cannot download movies, games, software, and music from Europe or Asia, like Pirate's Bay in Sweden. Although the U.S. government pressures foreign countries to go after internet pirates, the pirates relocate to countries with weak copyright laws.

Legislators are passing new, anti-capitalistic laws. For example, the State of Washington cracked down on house flipping. The state believes that house flippers renovate homes with substandard work and that they work in the underground economy. A new law requires a person buying a home to occupy the home for at least one year to re-sell it. If people plan to flip the property, they must register as contractors with the state or hire registered contractors. The state can fine any person violating this regulation $1,000 per day per job site, and several violations can result in criminal prosecution [5].

Nothing is wrong with buying, fixing, and selling a home for a higher price. That is capitalism! The government does not need to protect homebuyers because the market already provides a solution. A potential homebuyer can hire an inspector who thoroughly checks the home for problems and spots any shoddy, defective work. Unfortunately, registered contractors can also do poor work.

Legislators and Congressmen do not understand that strictly enforcing the law could create more criminals. For instance, many young people experiment with marijuana. During the 1960's, the government imposed fines for marijuana possession, and the conviction did not follow people throughout their lives. This was the good ole days before the arrival of massive computer databases. Now, some states have boosted the penalties for marijuana use. If a court convicts people of possessing marijuana, the judge can fine them, place them on probation, or sentence them to jail or prison.

The government strictly enforcing marijuana causes the following four problems:

> **Problem 1:** This person now has a criminal record. Most employers, including minimum-wage jobs, perform criminal background checks. Even if people quit smoking marijuana and can pass a drug test, they could have difficulties finding a job. Thus, this conviction follows them throughout their lives. Furthermore, the government bars people from careers in education, health care, and transportation [6].

> **Problem 2:** The government could bar people convicted of drug charges from federal financial aid for colleges and universities. With college tuition skyrocketing, many young people cannot afford to attend college without government assistance. Thus, people cannot attend college. Moreover, some colleges and universities expel violators [6].

> **Problem 3:** The government could bar convicted people from federal contracts, grants, and licenses [6]. Furthermore, the government may not allow people convicted of drug charges to enter the military. Before the 1960s, judges gave young defendants charged with minor crimes a choice: Join the military or go to jail. The military tends to take young, rebellious kids and turn them into young, respectable men.

> **Problem 4:** Many landlords check criminal records and could deny a convicted marijuana user a lease [6].

A person convicted of marijuana charges may not find suitable work, obtain an education, a place to live, an essential government license, or join the military. Which choices does this individual have? Instead of being a drug user, they can become a drug dealer.

Texas even stepped up the insanity. Prosecutors can enhance a misdemeanor to a felony charge for repeated offenders of simple marijuana possession. A felony charge in Texas is a death sentence because many institutions and employers check the Texas Department of Public Safety's database for criminal convictions. Convicted Texans could face a difficult time putting their lives back together and becoming law-abiding citizens. Unfortunately, the State of Texas funds a massive prison system in which the state continuously feeds inmates.

Above the Law

Lawmakers and politicians will pass thousands of laws, rules, and regulations and impose stringent penalties for violations. They portray themselves as saviors who must lead the flock of sheep along the righteous path. Our leaders embody the heart and soul of the Puritans. Unfortunately, these same politicians believe they are above the law and exempt themselves from their laws. Some politicians and lawmakers will violate their laws, rules, and regulations. If politicians are caught for a misdeed, they believe they can apologize and beg the public for forgiveness.

A wide variety of cases illustrates this message:

> **Case 1:** Former New York Governor Eliot Spitzer was busted for a clandestine arrangement with a prostitute. He was a New York State Attorney General and a tough prosecutor. He prosecuted Wall Street corruption and busted several prostitution rings [7].

> **Case 2:** The federal government indicted Rod R. Blagojevich, former Illinois governor, on 16 felony counts. The government believes Blagojevich tried to sell the U.S. Senate seat that President Barack Obama left vacant. Furthermore, Blagojevich supposedly squeezed campaign contributions from everyone by withholding state contracts,

granting regulatory favors, and filling state job vacancies with campaign contributors [8]. Blagojevich was a former prosecutor and helped write ethics laws for the State of Illinois.

> **Case 3:** William McCallum, a former assistant attorney general for the State of New Hampshire, was a kleptomaniac. He stole computers, paintings, and rare books from New England libraries, museums, and universities. A court sentenced McCallum to prison in 1998 [9].

Two factors explain why political leaders think they are above the law. First, politicians are greedy. They want to elevate themselves to the top social class in a materialistic society. Public servants do not earn high salaries, so they scheme, finding ways to elevate themselves. Moreover, political campaigns cost millions of dollars, and public servants must get this money from somewhere. Second, political leaders possess political power. Our political leaders believe they are better than everyone else and are entitled to numerous privileges.

For example, Congressmen do not collect social security when they retire. They voted for a much better plan. They earn their full salary until their death. Furthermore, Congressmen routinely exempt themselves from their laws. They do not abide by minimum wage laws, discrimination, and other laws. Congressmen are clever as they write laws. If we carefully read the federal laws, Congress lists all the parties that must comply with the law. However, Congressmen never list themselves and thus exempt themselves.

Some politicians and political insiders are not corrupt. However, they still form good ole-boy networks for two reasons. First, U.S. voters divide themselves on many issues equally. To get their agenda and laws passed, politicians form alliances with leaders and politicians from other groups. Politicians and political insiders form social clubs like college fraternities and sororities. Second, our laws, rules, and regulations are complicated. A complicated legal system makes bringing newcomers into the system difficult because newcomers require lots of time and patience. If a newcomer screws up the paperwork, then projects and money get delayed, creating headaches for government officials and bureaucrats. Working with the same people and organizations is simpler, thus forming these good ole boy networks.

No one enjoys paying taxes, including the politicians. However, political leaders hold a unique position. They know the government will not likely catch them if they evade taxes. How often does the Internal Revenue Service audit a President or Congressmen? Likewise, how often does a state tax authority audit a governor or legislator? These politicians pass laws that tax authorities must follow, and they appoint the leadership of the tax authorities. Consequently, these politicians know they can cheat on their taxes and not get caught. Nevertheless, tax agents can be brutal if they believe a citizen owes taxes.

President Obama illustrated this epidemic of tax evaders by filling positions in his government. Several of President Obama's choices had tax problems. First, Tim Geithner, the Treasury Secretary, did not pay Social Security and Medicare taxes when he worked for the International Monetary Fund (IMF) [10]. What makes this egregious is that the Internal Revenue Service collects these taxes, a department under the Department of Treasury. Second, Tom Daschle was nominated for director of Health and Human Services [11]. Third, Nancy Killefer was nominated for the chief performance officer. Fourth, Hilda Solis was nominated and appointed secretary of the Department of Labor [12]. Finally, Ron Kirk was nominated for the U.S. Trade Representative [13].

Now we understand why dead politicians easily win elections.

Corruption and the Government

Politicians and political leaders seek power. Once they attain power, they entrench themselves and expand their power [14]. This pursuit of power has always been there, but it took a turn for the worse in the last 30 years. Our leaders have become petty and puritanical. They believe they can meddle in any affair, regardless of circumstance, logic, or common sense. Our politicians and leaders of bureaucracies evolved into warlords who govern their piece of the pie with an iron fist.

What kind of leaders do we have in America? Our leaders share the following characteristics:

> **Characteristic 1:** Political leaders and government administrators despised being blamed for things going wrong [14]. They become experts at dodging blame, manipulating the truth, massive lies, and blaming others for our problems.

> **Characteristic 2:** Political leaders and government administrators are overly optimistic [14]. Every new law they pass and every government project makes society better. Of course, nobody analyzes the impact of the new rules or the government's projects. Leaders and administrators always propose new laws and projects and frown at anyone who examines the past. For instance, we experienced the 2007 Great Recession. Our leaders assured us the U.S. economy is recovering. However, it is already 2012, and no recovery has been in sight.

> **Characteristic 3:** Political leaders and government administrators use fear to expand their agenda and squelch the opposition. For example, politicians claim illegal immigrants traveling from Mexico carry drugs. Thus, states have the right to search anyone who appears to be an illegal immigrant. Furthermore, bullies utilize the internet and cell phones to perpetuate their bullying. Thus, school principals must have access to cell phones and email to stop this. On the other hand, police state marijuana is a gateway drug. One toke, and the next day, the users are injecting heroin into their veins. Finally, the government uses the ultimate fear – terrorism, to pass any law they want.

After government officials propagate these fears, the government can restrict rights, circumvent laws, and seize property without any questions, even if they have no basis for these fears. Consequently, our political leaders have significantly strengthened the government's dominion.

Alongside the growth of government is the explosion of corruption. This is no accident. Although corruption is difficult to define, we know corruption when we see it. Remembering that old saying, 'If it looks like a duck, walks like a duck, and quacks like a duck, then it is a duck.' Corruption thrives in societies with tyrants in the state and monopolies dominating a market.

Widespread corruption has four requirements:

> **Requirement 1:** A society needs moral loyalty and civic virtue to maintain itself. As a government becomes more corrupt, loyalty and virtue break down because people want their way. People, especially leaders, become hedonistic dogs with no moral constraints. They abuse their power to maintain their position and authority [15]. Ethics and loyalties have no place as leaders hold their positions of power.

> **Requirement 2:** Excessive inequality in wealth, power, and status exacerbates state corruption. As our leaders and wealthy climb to the top, they become selfish, proud, and arrogant. They do everything they can to maintain their position, even to the detriment of the people and society [15].

> **Requirement 3:** Society breaks down into warring factions. Factions are a source of wealth and power. Once a faction gains power, it influences the lawmakers, who in turn influence the laws. Then it uses the judicial and criminal justice systems to go after its opponents.

> **Requirement 4:** If bureaucrats receive low pay, have little chance of being caught, and have broad discretion to withhold essential permits or licenses, they are likely to be corrupt. Moreover, the government experiences problems extinguishing widespread corruption because corrupt bureaucrats will not report other corrupt bureaucrats.

Unfortunately, countries with severe corruption have difficulties reducing corruption because it has become a way of life and an acceptable business practice [16].

Has our society reached a point where corruption is a problem? Corporations dominate the economic activity in the United States. Although a corporation may not technically be a monopoly, it gains vast power over the government and our political leaders via campaign contributions. Moreover, civic loyalty is declining; inequality is rising while various factions are becoming more vocal. As these characteristics become more prevalent, then our society will develop these problems:

➢ Public law disintegrates and breaks down. People stop following the rules and become violators [15].

➢ Political debates lose meaning, logic, and common sense. Demagogues espouse class warfare and help one faction punish another faction [15].

➢ Violence becomes prevalent as people lose faith. Then the government has more difficulties reforming [15].

The methods to reduce corruption are simple. First, the government must reduce the concentration of power. For monopolies, the government breaks them up, regulates them, or exposes them to competition through international trade. Second, political leaders must reduce taxes and the size of government, eliminate subsidies, and reduce bureaucratic red tape. These policies break up a government's power. Unfortunately, governments rarely follow these policies. Instead, political leaders increase the size, scope, and mission of government to eliminate corruption. Hence, political leaders use more government to eliminate the problems of government.

Dividing the People

Politicians deliberately passed laws giving preferences to a gender, race, or social class. They claim the law addresses a previous injustice, but they artificially create factions. A faction helps cement an alliance between the politicians and the disadvantaged group. Sadly, the politicians pit the poor against the rich, women against men, minorities against white people, and children against adults, amplifying bitterness and hatred between different social groups.

The government pits the rich against the poor. Government leaders view the wealthy people in America as if they unfairly, illegally, or immorally earned their wealth. Politicians espouse this view because everyone views the rich as a source of tax revenue. For instance, many states have been experiencing severe financial difficulties since the 2008 Financial Crisis. Tax revenues are plummeting, so what is our government leaders' brilliant idea? Tax the Rich! This sounds like a simple solution, but it has three problems.

> **Problem 1:** The United States has a progressive tax system. Rich people already pay a higher proportion of taxes on their incomes, so imposing greater taxes on the wealthy only penalizes them more.

> **Problem 2:** Rich people relocate to states or countries with low tax burdens. A state over-taxing the rich can hurt itself financially if the wealthy people flee to another state or country.

> **Problem 3:** States over-relied on the rich for tax revenue. For example, Wall Street was flush with cash and high salaries. With the financial markets crash in September 2008, many rich financial people earned losses, causing New York to have a $13.7 billion deficit for 2009-2010 [17]. California had an estimated deficit of $42 billion for 2009 [18].

Nothing is wrong with being rich. Being rich ultimately rewards someone for providing a valuable good or service to society. For instance, Bill Gates started Microsoft in a rundown motel in New Mexico. Steve Wozniak and Steve Jobs began Apple computers in their garage in California, and Michael Dell started Dell Computers in his dorm room at the University of Texas. Even if people inherit their wealth, they must remain vigilant and still work. If they make a wrong investment decision or hire an accountant who steals them blind, then these rich people could end up on the streets as homeless. True social mobility works in both directions. Some poor people can become rich, while some wealthy can become poor.

State laws for domestic violence pit women against men. Daily TV commercials inform women that all men are violent and that they must report any violence to the police. Of course, states established special courts to hear domestic violence cases and encourage the police to arrest all males suspected of domestic violence. Several states can charge a person with domestic violence, even with the absence of physical contact. For example, in Oklahoma, a couple arguing in front of a child has committed domestic violence. However, women never perpetrate violence. Police always arrest the males.

Domestic violence laws are not bad. If a partner physically hurts his mate, then the police should arrest him or her. However, the police arrested the males for a scratch on an arm, or the couple argued in front of a child. Some judges fail to understand that some women will falsely accuse a man of domestic violence in some instances. For example, if a woman wants to divorce her husband, a false domestic charge swings the divorce decree in her favor. Moreover, a woman becomes angry with her mate and seeks revenge by alleging domestic violence. Consequently, some men believe they became slaves to women. Once a woman is done with a man, she can call the state and have him removed. Then the woman legally steals all his assets.

A question naturally arises. Why do courts and police fret over minor cases of domestic violence? The answer should not surprise us. Most criminals do not have money, and the government expends resources to arrest, convict, and house criminals. Unfortunately, families are a source of income and wealth. Most family men will bond out of jail and return to their mate. Then the courts encourage the males to plead guilty and pay court fines and fees, counseling, and other services.

Sexual harassment is dividing men and women. The theory of sexual harassment is employees in the workplace should be free from sexual advances or objectionable material. Common sense defines the following as sexual harassment.

> ➢ Repeatedly asking a co-worker for a date or constantly flirting with a co-worker who does not like it.

> ➢ Forcing a co-worker to engage in sexual activity as a condition for employment or advancement.

> ➢ Telling sexual jokes or displaying sexual material.

The Equal Employment Opportunity Commission (EEOC) defines sexual harassment as "verbal or physical conduct of a sexual nature [that] unreasonably interferes with an individual's work performance or creates an intimidating, hostile, or offensive work environment." Sadly, lawyers interpret this law broadly. For example, women sue men over unwanted stares in California. Thus, more lawsuits could arise. Could a man sue a woman if she wears provocative clothes? Will the EEOC initiate dress codes to stop unwanted stares? Unfortunately, the government can construe any conflict between males and females as sexual harassment.

Sexual harassment laws are dividing males and females in the workplace and negatively impacting the work environment. Political correctness dictates that men sexually harass women. Thus, many men are afraid to ask a woman for a date in the workplace or tell a joke that is taken out of context. Furthermore, some women can falsely accuse a male worker to get the male in trouble or fired. Employers are afraid of sexual harassment claims. A woman could sue the male and her employer if she could show that the company did not take her accusation seriously. Consequently, managers take the easy solution and fire males if any conflicts arise between genders.

The anti-discrimination laws are pitting whites against the minority groups. The United States was wrong for allowing slavery to flourish in the South. The next step is to move society towards a system that does not look at a person's race. Martin Luther King stated it best, "my four children will one day live in a nation where they will not be judged by the color of their skin but by the content of their character." A way to eliminate racial discrimination is for everyone to become color-blind concerning skin color. However, the federal and state governments went in the opposite direction.

Federal and state governments require employers to collect racial information on applicants. Then the government can deny a grant or sue a business if it appears racist. Thus, a business does not want to appear racist, so it hires minorities, which it calls tokens. Although this may be against the spirit of the law, an employment recruiter can find reasons to reject a white applicant's application but discount negative information in a minority applicant's application. Finally, minority workers who are fired can sue and claim discrimination.

Discrimination laws create a split in the law. Employers cannot use race to hire or promote employees. However, a university admissions office can accept applicants based on race [19]. If every applicant has similar qualifications, an employer or university can always choose a minority, which is not necessarily bad. Nevertheless, many white males feel they are at the bottom of the applicant pool despite their qualifications and education, creating bitter feelings between white males and everyone else.

Laws are pitting children against adults. Rules and regulations have become so stringent that parents and school officials cannot spank children. If a state allows spanking, then it enforces many restrictions. Kids know this! If a parent, teacher, or principal lays any hand on them, they know they can call the police and have that person arrested. The law treats all kids as little darlings who can do no wrong. Moreover, the police detained teachers and principals for restraining kids after catching the kids fighting [20].

Police aggressively going after the parents, teachers, and principals will cause three impacts:

> **Impact 1:** Parents will not discipline their children because they fear the state will arrest them. Consequently, behavioral problems in children will worsen.

> **Impact 2:** Laws have a chilling effect on teachers [20]. Teachers will avoid breaking up fights or getting involved. Otherwise, the police can arrest them. Kids know this and may become more disruptive.

> **Impact 3:** Crazy laws and overzealous enforcement of laws will drive good teachers out of education and other occupations dealing with children. Why remain in an occupation that pays the lowest for college graduates? Children can be disruptive, and the state will go after anyone if it thinks the person did something wrong. Thus, education will continually decline as kids become more disruptive as good teachers flee the schools.

Education is a coercive process. Students must sit at a desk and study material they typically would not study independently. Kids usually have a favorite class but must learn material for classes they do not like. Remember the old phrase, "Spare the rod and spoil the child." If we cater to a child, they will not learn discipline or study complex subjects. Unfortunately, children do not appreciate an education until they have reached 30 and started their careers. Then they wished they had studied harder in school.

Complicated U.S. Laws

The current U.S. legal system has evolved into a highly complicated system. U.S. federal, state, county, and city governments can create and alter laws. Unfortunately, these laws occupy volumes upon volumes of books that span a whole floor in a public library. Sadly, we have so many laws in the United States that we cannot know them all!

The travesty of our complex legal system is that the government expands the number of enforcers. If the government catches a person violating any laws, the government can seize a person's property, impose hefty fines, and incarcerate the person. Everybody is a potential criminal with millions of rules, regulations, and ordinances on the books. Thus, government at all levels must continuously scrutinize their citizens. Everyone has heard of these cases:

> **Case 1:** Code enforcement monitors people's property for violations. The local government goes after homeowners if their grass grows too high, or they start a home business, such as a daycare or car repair. Of course, many communities have homeowners associations, which are just as bad as the government.

> **Case 2:** Child-Protective Services immediately invade a family's home if someone reports any child abuse. Some people seek revenge and lie to investigators. Investigators do not know who tells the truth or who lies. Therefore, the state could remove kids from innocent parents from a false accusation. Then the innocent parents must spend money on a lawyer to get the children back.

> **Case 3:** A person sitting on his couch, watching TV, and drinking a beer has violated a law. If a cop sees this behavior through a window, the state can charge that person for public intoxication.

Why did the legal system become so complicated? Let us start with the federal government. The U.S. Constitution and the Bill of Rights are the premier documents establishing the federal government. The government changes the Federal law for the following:

> **Creating New Laws:** Congress and the President sign new laws, which they write into the United States Code. These new laws should not conflict with previous laws or violate people's rights as defined in the Bill of Rights.

> **Interpreting the Laws:** All federal bureaucracies must adhere to the United States Code. However, Congress usually writes vague, confusing laws. Thus, each federal agency must interpret the laws' meaning and record their interpretations in their law books, which we call the Federal Code of Regulations (CFR). Every agency maintains its own CFRs and interprets the United States Code differently.

> **Modifying the Laws:** The federal court system also interprets, defines, and modifies the laws. Of course, the court system can put its unique spin on federal regulations.

Congress and the President passing laws create the following problems:

> **Problem 1:** These laws span hundreds of pages. For example, the Energy Independence and Security Act of 2007 contains 311 pages with standard margins and 12-point font [21]. Unfortunately, Congress typically passes these types of laws.

> **Problem 2:** Many Congressmen do not read the laws before voting on them. An organization, Downsize DC, proposes a new law requiring all Congressmen to read their laws before they vote for them. More information about the organization is available at www.downsizedc.org.

> **Problem 3:** When a country experiences a crisis, the U.S. President bullies Congress into passing laws. For example, President Bush forced Congress to pass the Patriot Act after the terrorist attack on September 11, 2001, and the Troubled

Asset Relief Program to bail out Wall Street and the large banks caught in the 2008 Financial Crisis.

> **Problem 4:** Congress can only agree on a law if it boosts their salaries or restricts U.S. citizens' rights. For example, the Tea Party and Wall Street Protestors rose to challenge and change the government. Congressmen despise publicity and do not want to lose an election. Therefore, they passed the Federal Restricted Buildings and Grounds Improvement Act of 2011, which makes protests a felony. If a protestor is standing near a location protected by the Secret Service (anywhere), the federal government can subsequently charge a protestor with a felony. Another law, Congress and the President passed the National Defense Authorization Act (NDAA) in 2012, which allows the military to detain a U.S. citizen indefinitely without a jury trial.

These laws violate the U.S. Bill of Rights. The First Amendment to the Constitution states, "the right of the people peaceably to assemble, and to petition the Government for a redress of grievances." The Fifth Amendment to the Constitution states, "In all criminal prosecutions, the accused shall enjoy the right to a speedy and public trial, by an impartial jury of the State and district wherein the crime shall have been committed." Consequently, our new laws violate the U.S. Bill of Rights, so we conclude our laws have become arbitrary and egregious. Congress and the President can pass any law they want and suffer no consequences.

State, county, and city governments replicated the U.S. federal government. They continually create new laws and reinterpret old ones. Consequently, how does the government know people are following the rules? Unfortunately, enforcers complement our laws. As the legal system expands, the government must hire more enforcers to ensure people follow the laws. Unfortunately, the government demands results, and enforcers must find violators, proving they are working hard. They believe these laws are making society a better place to live.

Conclusion

Our politicians continuously pass new laws to cure everybody's problems or to protect the public from all the evil in this world. Unfortunately, bad, evil things happen to good, honest people all the time and will continue to happen to good, honest people all the time. Leaders stacking law upon law will not help the economy, will not help businesses thrive, and will not help job growth. Instead, continual expansion of complex laws will produce these negative consequences:

> ➢ **Consequence 1:** The government must expand bureaucracies to enforce these laws. Consequently, government employs more bureaucrats in the federal, state, and local governments over time. Thus, society must pay higher taxes, fees, and fines for these bureaucracies, which hurl more hardship on the private sector.

> ➢ **Consequence 2:** More complicated laws mean the government finds more people violating the rules. Therefore, the criminal justice system continually expands over time, diverting public funds from other investments, such as education and infrastructure.

> ➢ **Consequence 3:** Businesses and citizens must hire legal specialists and consultants to interpret and keep laws compliant. Specialists and consultants are expensive, which increases businesses' costs. Businesses pass these higher costs onto the consumers as higher prices for goods and services. Consequently, a complicated legal structure expands the industries for compliance specialists while other industries, such as the U.S. manufacturing industry, contract.

Unfortunately, people earning their living from the legal system will fight against de-regulation or simplification of the rules. For example, the overly complicated tax code has given birth to a whole industry of tax accountants, consultants, and computer software companies. If the government simplified the tax system by imposing a flat tax, the tax industry would fight the change.

The decriminalization of marijuana represents another example. The criminal justice system would see fewer cases for marijuana and would contract because marijuana violations comprise a significant portion of court cases.

The government expansion of drug laws in the 1960s fueled the massive growth of federal and state prisons. If the federal and state governments decriminalize drug use, our leaders could cut the criminal justice system in half. Many judges, lawyers, prison guards, and police would become unemployed. Instead, they scare the public about an imminent crime wave if we decriminalize some behavior.

References

[1] Chico Municipal Code. "Nuclear Free Zone Law." Division IX – Nuclear Weapons, Chapter 9.60. Accessed on (5/15/08) at ttp://www.chico.ca.us/municipal_code/title_9.pdf

[2] Pacific Grover Municipal Code. " Monarch Butterflies." Title 11 Health, Safety, and Environment, Chapter 48.010. Accessed on (5/20/08) at http://www.ci.pg.ca.us/

[3] Rogers, John. May 15, 2008. "In L.A., controversy sizzles over taco truck restrictions." *Houston Chronicle*.

[4] Lieberman, Joe. April 26, 2001. "The Media Marketing Accountability Act." Available at http://lieberman.senate.gov/newsroom/release.cfm?id=208614 (access date 01/12/09).

[5] Howell, Parker, May 29, 2008. "House flipping now can draw hefty fines." *Spokesman Review*.

[6] Aho, Karen. November 27, 2007. "The Basics: What illegal drug use can cost you." *MSNBC*

[7] Arena, Kelli and John King. March 11, 2008. "Source: Spitzer investigated for link to prostitution ring." *CNN Politics.com*

[8] Coen, Jeff. April 3, 2009. "Former Gov. Rod Blagojevich indicted." *Los Angeles Times*.

[9] Associated Press. December 16, 2008. "Former NH lawyer stops payments for art thefts." *Auction Central News*.

[10] Wolf, Bryon. January 26, 2009. "Senate Approves Geithner Despite Tax Issues." *ABC News*. Available at http://abcnews.go.com/Politics/President44/story?id=6733907&page=1 (access date 05/15/09).

[11] Freking, Kevin. February 2, 2009. "Daschle apologizes for failure to pay $120,000 in taxes." *Houston Chronicle.*

[12] Kelley, Matt. February 5, 2009. "Tax snafus add up for Obama team." *USA Today*. Available at http://www.usatoday.com/news/washington/2009-02-05-solis-husband-taxes_N.htm (access date 05/15/09).

[13] Murray, Mark. March 2, 2009. "More tax problems for Team Obama?" *MSNBC*. Available at http://firstread.msnbc.msn.com/archive/2009/03/02/1817065.aspx (access date 05/15/09).

[14] Morgan, Theodore. 1964. "The Theory of Error in Centrally-Directed Economic Systems." *The Quarterly Journal of Economics* 78(3): 395-419.

[15] Dobel. J. Patrick. 1978. "The Corruption of a State." *The American Political Science Review* 72(3): 958-973

[16] Aidt, Toke S. 2003. "Review: Economic Analysis of Corruption: A Survey." *The Economic Journal* 113(491): F632-F652.

[17] WBNG News. December 16, 2008. "Governor Paterson's Executive Budget." *WBNG.*

[18] Christie, Jim. December 11, 2008. "California budget shortfall seen nearing $42 billion." *Reuters*

[19] Trachtman, Michael G. 2003. "Is There Anything Wrong With Favoring Minorities To Promote Diversity In Your Workplace?" *NewsletterAccess.com*. Available at http://www.newsletteraccess.com/display_article.php?id=10099 (access date: 12/24/08).

[20] Pape, John. 2008. "Principal Claims Innocence, Says His Arrest Sends Wrong Signal." *Fort Bend Now*. Available at www.fortbendnow.com (access date 07/03/08).

[21] U.S. Government Printing Office. 2007. Energy Independence and Security Act of 2007. Washington, DC: Available at http://purl.access.gpo.gov/GPO/LPS94451 (access date 10/21/08).

3. Frivolous Lawsuits

"It's strange that men should take up crime when there are so many legal ways to be dishonest."

-Author Unknown

Every country developed a codified law system defining the legal relationships between people, businesses, and government. We define codified laws into four types:

- ➤ **English Common Law System:** All former English colonies except Malta have this system, including Australia, Canada, Hong Kong, India, Great Britain, and the United States.

- ➤ **Civil Law System:** The civil law system is one of the oldest and most dominant legal systems, originating from the ancient Roman Empire. Most European and Latin American countries use a civil system. They adopted either the Napoleonic or Germanic civil code.

- ➤ **A Religious Legal System:** Religion becomes the inspiration and source of law. All Christian nations have moved away from a religious legal system. However, several Muslim countries still follow a Muslim religious legal system known as Sharia Law.

- ➤ **A Hybrid System:** A country mixes religious and common law, or religious and civil law.

The United States has a standard law system, whereas the court system provides additional checks and balances on the other two branches of government. Congress and the President can sign new laws into existence, and the court system can shape these laws. If Congress and the President pass a bad law, a court can remove it through judicial review or reshape it.

Common law creates the following benefits:

> **Benefit 1:** Courts provide an additional check on the government. Most states and the federal government appoint judges free from the voters' whim. Judges do not seek re-election or appease the voters. Some states, such as Michigan, Oklahoma, and Texas, elect judges for public office. Are judges in these states serving justice or running popularity contests?

> **Benefit 2:** English common law is flexible. Judges can reshape laws as society changes.

> **Benefit 3:** English common law uses jury trials. Jury trials provide an immense check on the legal system. Attorneys on both sides of a trial present their case in front of an impartial jury, a group of people from society. Consequently, attorneys must research to sway a jury to their side.

The standard law system has three disadvantages.

> **Disadvantage 1:** If Congress and the President signed a lousy law into existence, the court system has to wait for a court case challenging the bad law. The court system does not immediately strike down bad laws. If it did, it would have enormous power. Thus, bad laws can be in the law books for years before the courts remove them.

> **Disadvantage 2:** The common law system is more complex. Judges refer to the laws passed by Congress and the President and court cases that set legal precedents. A precedent is a critical court case that starts a new interpretation of the law or reshapes old laws.

> **Disadvantage 3:** The government appoints judges based on their political views rather than their abilities.

All states replicated the common law system except Louisiana, which adopted a civil system based on the Napoleonic code. Judges in a civil law system strictly enforce the law and cannot alter it. Consequently, a civil court judge enforces all conditions of a contract, while a common-law judge can modify contracts. Finally, a civil law judge or a panel of judges is the sole decider in civil systems. However, some countries with civil systems have incorporated juries.

High-income countries usually have a common law system, although civil law dominates the world. Table 1 shows the top 10 income per capita countries with their type of legal system. Bermuda, Brunei, Falkland Islands, Hong Kong, Jersey, and Liechtenstein have a British Common Law System, while Singapore and Qatar mix common and religious legal systems. The United States was in the top ten, but its ranking continually dropped. Consequently, the wealthiest countries in the world have a common law system.

Table 1: The Richest Countries in the World in 2011

Country	GDP per capita	Legal System
Liechtenstein	$141,100	English Common Law System
Qatar	$102,700	Common and Religious Law
Luxembourg	$84,700	Civil Code – Napoleonic Code
Bermuda	$69,900	English Common Law System
Singapore	$59,900	Common and Religious Law
Jersey	$57,000	English Common Law System
Falkland Islands	$55,400	English Common Law System
Norway	$53,000	Scandinavian-German Civil Law
Brunei	$49,400	English Common Law System
Hong Kong	$49,300	English Common Law System

Sources: 2007 Central Intelligence Agency – The World Factbook; Wikipedia – Legal Systems of the World

Common law systems usually have strong, pro-business legal systems. Furthermore, common-law judges have shown leadership and initiative by using a court case to reshape society. Two famous examples are:

> ➤ Example 1: The Bill of Rights originally applied to the federal government. However, the Supreme Court expanded the Bill of Rights to the states through the case of Gitlow

versus New York (1925). The State of New York arrested and convicted Gitlow for criminal anarchy because Gitlow was a socialist who advocated the overthrow of the government. Gitlow wrote his views in his "Left Wing Manifesto" and was caught distributing these pamphlets to the public. The Supreme Court ruled the State of New York did not violate Gitlow's right to free speech or freedom of the press because his writings advocated the overthrow of the government.

> **Example 2:** After the North won the Civil War, President Abraham Lincoln freed the slaves in the South. However, the large plantation owners relied on slavery as cheap labor. Thus, the southern state governments initiated a new system that perpetuated slavery without calling it slavery, which we know as the "Separate but Equal Laws." The South separated African-Americans and whites if the state provided equal facilities for both races. Consequently, African Americans had different facilities for schools, restrooms, and parks and separate seating for buses and restaurants. Of course, African Americans were short-changed and given inferior facilities and schooling.

Laws kept them poor and imprisoned on the plantations. In 1954, the Supreme Court removed the Separate but Equal Laws in Brown versus Board of Education of Topeka, Kansas. Thus, the Supreme Court legally ended segregation and initiated the civil rights movement.

Common-law judges did great things for our country and helped improve society. However, our contemporary judges and Supreme Court justices possess a pro-government attitude. They expand government and restrict citizens' rights. Two prominent examples are:

> **Example 1:** Supreme Court intervened in the 2000 Presidential Election. The election between George W. Bush and Al Gore was very close; one state, Florida, became the

deciding factor. Bush [supposedly] beat Gore by several hundred votes. The Supreme Court halted the recount of punch-card ballots in Florida because a recount would violate George Bush's right to the "equal protection of the laws." Justices voted in a 5-4 decision [1]. Did the conservatives on the Supreme Court stand behind Bush because he was conservative, or did they truly protect Bush's rights? What happened to the rights of Al Gore?

> **Example 2:** The U.S. Congress and the President passed the Clean Air Act of 1990, which gave the Environment Protection Agency (EPA) the legal authority to regulate pollution emissions of 188 chemicals.

Public awareness of global warming has focused attention on carbon dioxide emissions. Consequently, the U.S. Supreme Court ruled in Massachusetts versus the EPA (2006) that the EPA must regulate carbon dioxide as a pollutant.

The Supreme Court ruling has two problems. First, the original law never included carbon dioxide as a pollutant, but the Supreme Court added this to the law. Second, the cycle of life requires carbon dioxide. Humans and animals breathe out carbon dioxide, while plants recycle the carbon and create oxygen.

Supreme Court ruling vastly expands the EPA's sphere of power. All humans and animals, using fossil fuels such as gasoline, diesel, and coal, emit carbon dioxide. In the EPA's defense, they were sued to add carbon dioxide. They did not actively seek out this additional responsibility. However, the court has given the EPA vast authority over the U.S. economy [2].

Massachusetts sued the EPA because computer simulation models showed the Massachusetts' coast could be underwater in 50 years. However, global warming is a theory! We do not know if we are experiencing a warming trend or if greenhouse gases like carbon dioxide are warming the earth. Scientists who build these models program their beliefs into the computer model. If the scientists believe in global warming, their models will reflect that. Economists built large simulation models of the economy during the 1960s, but they stopped making them. The models provide poor economic forecasts. Now, they make these models to model pollution for the whole planet!

Pundits of global warming ignore active sunspots. A more active sun may warm the earth. For instance, the 17th century experienced little sunspot activity; historians call this the mini-Ice Age. Moreover, if we were around in the 1960s, the fear for humanity was the dawn of a new Ice Age because the world experienced a slight cooling trend.

Torts

A common law system is a strong system if good judges with common sense fill the courts. Common-law judges established and defined the modern laws for property rights, contract law, and torts. A tort occurs when one person or party harms another party. Then a judge or jury compensates the victim for the harm.

Judges can use torts to compensate people efficiently for harm. Compensation makes the harmed party "whole again," so the harmed party is just as well off as if the harm did not occur. The problem is that "whole again" is a value judgment. For example, a person owned a car for five years until his relative wrecked the vehicle. A person has used the car for five years, so "whole again" does not mean he should get a new car. He only gets the car's current value at the time of the accident. Consequently, harmed parties over-appraise the harm, while the harmer (tortfeasor) undervalues the harm. Judges or juries must determine if the plaintiff is at fault, and if they are, then place a value on the harm.

Torts arise from the following three situations:

> One party harms another party intentionally. These harms are usually crimes, such as assault, attempted murder, or murder.

> One party accidentally harms another party. This harm could be a crime in cases such as manslaughter, maiming, or causing a permanent injury.

> A defective product harms one party accidentally.

Modern courts have expanded the definition of harm. Judges apply tort laws to parties who are not responsible. Moreover, judges and juries can add punitive damages to the compensation. Punitive damages punish the plaintiff for the harm, thus teaching him a lesson.

Four prominent examples show the problems with torts:

> **Example 1:** Judges and juries need help placing an actual value on the harm. Hence, every harm is inflated to a million dollars or more. In one case, Pennzoil versus Texaco, the court initially awarded $11.12 billion in damages and $1 billion in punitive damages [3]. Thus, one lawsuit can easily bankrupt a company or a small corporation.

> **Example 2:** Courts include mental anguish and suffering as damages. Judges and juries already have difficulties valuing harm, but now they must place a value on suffering. Of course, defendants receive damages as money, so they have an incentive to exaggerate their suffering.

> **Example 3:** Courts expand cause and effect. Tort should remain close to the affected parties at hand. For instance, a drunk driver harmed an innocent bystander because he drove while intoxicated. A drunk driver committed a crime, and an injured innocent bystander has every right to sue for damages. However, alcoholics usually do not have money, so attorneys follow the alcohol and pursue the parties with money, such as bars or liquor stores. If a bar or store did not sell the alcohol, then the innocent bystander would not be harmed.

The problem is, where does the chain of causality stop? In this case, the chain of causality is the drunk caused the harm (immediate), but the drunk drank alcohol; the store sold the alcohol to the drunk; a company sold the alcohol to the store; the farmers sold the ingredients to the company to make alcohol, and God created the yeasts that convert the sugars in grains into alcohol. Lawyers can follow the causality chain well until they reach a party with deep pockets. Fortunately, the court system cannot access God's checkbook; otherwise, all the lawyers would sue God since he starts at the beginning of all causality chains.

> **Example 4:** Courts do not assign responsibility correctly and ignore the notion of free choice. For example, everybody knows which foods are healthy and which are not. We all know fast food is not healthy food. However, two teenagers sued McDonald's in New York, blaming McDonald's for their weight gain and health problems.

McDonald's did not force anyone at gunpoint to eat their food. Teenagers freely choose which foods to eat and which place. McDonald's sells good salads, too, but consumers do not line up to buy salads. Surprisingly, the court correctly dismissed the lawsuit. Remember, McDonald's still hired attorneys to fight his lawsuit, which costs money. If McDonald's lost, then attorneys would file hundreds of lawsuits against McDonald's. Once a piranha tastes blood, they swarm in and devour the victim.

The rise of frivolous torts and lawsuits is leading to a crisis in America. Innocent parties can be sued for the most ridiculous reasons. Out-of-control lawsuits can harm the U.S. economy. Lawsuits expropriate money from businesses and families and could cause bankruptcies. Furthermore, some people are compelled to play the lawsuit lottery game. The public knows many high-profile lawsuits in which defendants win millions of dollars from a court case. Some people injure themselves to tilt the lawsuit in their favor. Some examples include the following:

> **Example 1:** Some obstetricians switched their specialties to lower-risk ones. If a doctor accidentally harms a patient, an insurance company pays compensation to the patient. Thus, all doctors must carry malpractice insurance. Unfortunately,

these doctors are hit with many lawsuits and large damage awards. Insurance companies hiked the premiums. For example, one doctor, who was never sued, saw his malpractice insurance jump to $84,000 per year in 2004. He only paid $23,000 in 2002 [4]. Consequently, obstetricians can no longer afford their malpractice insurance and switch specialties rather than fight a wave of lawsuits. A shortage of obstetricians is so severe that pregnant mothers drive to the next county or the nearest largest city to find an obstetrician.

➤ **Example 2:** The most infamous case is the McDonald's coffee lawsuit. In 1992, Stella Liebeck and her grandson bought breakfast from the drive-thru at McDonald's. Her grandson parked the car, allowing Stella to add cream and sugar to her coffee. She accidentally spilled coffee on her lap, causing third-degree burns. Stella stayed in the hospital for two weeks and required skin grafts. Pain and suffering were real, but this case's problem starts with the definition of a tort. Stella burned herself, which was not McDonald's fault. If a person accidentally hurts himself, then it is their fault, not somebody else. Her lawyer claimed McDonald's sold a harmful product because McDonald's coffee tends to be hotter than other restaurants. A jury awarded Stella $2.86 million, but the trial judge lowered the amount to $640,000. McDonald's and Stella settled for a lower, undisclosed amount [5].

➤ **Example 3:** A federal judge sued a dry cleaner for $65 million because the dry cleaner lost his pants. A week later, the dry cleaner found the pants. Dry cleaners were from Seoul, South Korea, and came to this country to live the American dream. The owners have become disenchanted with the U.S. legal system. They are considering returning to South Korea [6].

> **Example 4:** A woman wanted to sue Wendy's restaurants because she found a severed human finger in her chili. Police discovered the woman planted the finger in the chili, hoping to be compensated by Wendy's. This woman also has a history of filing lawsuits. Unfortunately, this incident tarnished Wendy's reputation, which persists to this day [7].

These substantial damage awards have attracted schools of sharks to the legal profession. These schools of sharks swim around the economy, searching for victims with money. We call these sharks lawyers, and lawsuits are profitable, or at least until the 2008 Financial Crisis. Even law firms are laying off attorneys, so the 2008 financial crisis has one positive aspect.

Out-of-control lawsuits impose five problems on a society.

> **Problem 1:** Lawsuits are expensive. A company spends thousands of dollars to fight a frivolous lawsuit.

> **Problem 2:** Some companies have multiple lawsuits filed against them. For example, Wal-Mart is fighting 5,000 lawsuits. Wal-Mart pays an immense legal bill as it sends lawyers across the United States to file paperwork with the courts.

> **Problem 3:** All organizations, even small ones, hire one or more attorneys. Attorneys give legal advice to the managers, but they do not produce goods and services. Thus, businesses must hire people who do not contribute directly to the bottom line.

> **Problem 4:** Large damage awards can bankrupt businesses or force a company to flee to a country with a more hospitable legal environment.

> **Problem 5:** Lawsuits can halt economic development. For example, local government and most citizens want a company to build a factory in their community. The factory

will bring jobs, create wealth, and expand the tax base, boosting local tax revenues. One person can halt this progress by filing a lawsuit against the company, stopping economic development.

The Festering Growth of Attorneys

The United States has an unbelievably complex legal system. With too many laws, people outside the legal profession need help understanding or following them. An overly complex legal system automatically creates a demand for lawyers. Of course, lawyers cannot remember all the laws, so lawyers specialize in the typical specialties of criminal, civil, divorce, immigration, or tax. Why do we have so many laws? Lawyers pack Congress and the state legislatures. They dream up new rules or expand old ones, strengthening the legal profession.

According to the American Bar Association, in 2008, the United States had 1,162,124 practicing attorneys. This statistic does not include law school graduates who do not practice law. Furthermore, the number of practicing attorneys increased by 18,000 in 2007. This number appears small compared to the U.S. population of approximately 300 million Americans. However, the U.S. has one lawyer for every 300 men, women, and children.

The U.S. economy is teeming with ravenous attorneys. Attorneys provide legal services, such as suing people and businesses for money. If the United States had one lawyer for every 300 men, women, and children, then a lawyer would have few options. A lawyer works at least 40 hours a week for 52 weeks per year. Consequently, attorneys are creative in filing lawsuits, dreaming of new ways of extorting money from businesses and people or creating a demand for their services.

Attorneys utilize six standard methods to extort money from innocent parties:

> **Method 1:** An attorney files a nuisance lawsuit. A lawyer can sue someone for a silly reason, but the high cost of preparing and going to trial forces the defendant to settle out

of court. Some people and businesses have principles and will fight any lawsuit regardless of the amount of money. Thus, the defendants will hire a lawyer or a team of lawyers to fight the lawsuit.

➤ **Method 2:** Lawyers are not incentivized to finish work because they charge by the hour. During a lawsuit, the plaintiffs and defendants have lawyers with a financial incentive to delay the court case, racking up more time and larger legal bills. Thus, lawyers love messy cases because chaotic cases involve time and are expensive.

➤ **Method 3:** Lawyers pick the courts where they want their cases heard. Some court districts are located in regions where judges and jurors favor the plaintiffs.

➤ **Method 4:** An attorney files a lawsuit against a person for failure to repay a debt. If the person does not attend court, the judge automatically grants a default judgment in the lawyer's favor. Now, the lawyer can schedule another hearing to garnish wages or seize a bank account. Lawyers can be dirty if the attorney sends the notice to appear in court to the wrong address or a previous address, ensuring the person does not appear for the hearing. Judges held innocent people responsible for debts that were not theirs.

➤ **Method 5:** Class-action lawsuits provide ample financial compensation to lawyers, even for minor harms. For example, if a lawyer has one client with a $1,000 lawsuit, the lawyer may earn 40% or $400 if they win. This represents a small financial incentive. However, if the lawyer can represent 1,000 clients simultaneously for $400 per client, his stake rises to $400,000. Thus, this lawsuit becomes worth the time and effort.

➤ **Method 6:** Some lawyers establish rackets. For example, an attorney finds two people with good car insurance and artificially causes a car accident. Then the lawyer sends the people to his network of doctors, who find whiplash and other injuries. Next, the lawyer files a claim or sues the car insurance companies for damages. The doctor, attorney, and clients get a cut of the insurance check. Unfortunately, everyone in society pays greater insurance premiums.

The Parasitic Class

A government with an overly complicated legal system creates a parasitic class. A parasitic class represents a group of people who depend on the government for their livelihood. We may think that people on welfare and other social programs belong to the parasitic class. However, the parasitic class depends on a person's circumstances. If the recipients use government aid temporarily, they are not in the parasitic class. They use government as a crutch to get them back on their feet. This is why the government provides social programs. Nevertheless, if people can work and depend on the government for aid for a lifetime with no intentions ever to give it up, then they are parasites.

Unfortunately, the United States may have a sizeable parasitic class because our social programs have the following problems:

> **Problem 1:** The government freely hands out money. Some people will purposely change their circumstances or lie to get government aid. For example, a person lies about a back problem to get disability pay. A mother on welfare avoids marriage or obtains a divorce to collect a welfare check. Despite any government crackdown, freeloaders who do not need the aid will always take advantage of free help. Always! One shocking observation about our economy is the large number of young people who look healthy but have a disability. Once the government says a person is disabled, they can collect a monthly check for the rest of their lives.

> **Problem 2:** The government provides the wrong incentives. For instance, state welfare programs give more money to

single mothers with more children. Consequently, single mothers bear more children to collect larger welfare checks. Unfortunately, the children see their mother receiving free money, which encourages them to do poorly in school and not acquire any skills. They know they can get welfare, too, once they reach 18 and have children. Thus, government programs encourage single-parent households and continue a cycle of dependence for the next generation.

> **Problem 3:** Government programs create dependence on aid. Many people on aid do not upgrade their skills or search for a job. For instance, what is our salary threshold to start working if we receive $15,000 a year from the government to do nothing? Would we start working for $30,000 per year? The problem is that we work and must pay taxes from that salary. That salary threshold can be pretty high for most people.

> **Problem 4:** Government programs divert funding away from charity organizations. People contribute less to charities because their taxes help support social programs. Of course, if the government levies hefty taxes on people's incomes to finance these public programs, then people are rarely in a charitable mood.

Nothing is wrong with social programs. The government needs a more innovative approach. An excellent social program requires two components. First, the aid must be temporary. Second, the program must wean the recipients of the assistance. Remember the adage: If we give a man a fish, he can eat for a day. If we teach a man how to fish, he can feed himself for a lifetime.

One exception is Social Security. Many countries give senior citizens income security because the government rewards older people for being taxpayers for most of their lives. Of course, senior citizens are a strong voting group that career politicians must cater to.

The parasitic class is much larger and includes several groups of professionals, such as lawyers and bureaucrats, who depend on the government for their employment and livelihood. They thrive on complicated laws and rules and, in turn, earn high salaries for their knowledge. Five examples illustrate how professionals are parasites feeding off society.

> **Example 1:** With the government welfare programs, the government hires counselors, attorneys, psychologists, and other professionals who determine who gets aid and how much. If the states did not have these programs, these professionals would not be employed in the government.

> **Example 2:** Lawyers represent a large group of parasites. If the rules and laws were simple, then families and businesses would not need the services of lawyers. However, U.S. and state laws are extremely complicated and beyond the comprehension of most people. Thus, they hire one or many attorneys. Lawyers even hire lawyers to win lawsuits. Furthermore, judges always recommend that defendants retain lawyers, and they frown at people representing themselves.

> **Example 3:** The government will deny the claims for half the people who apply for Social Security. Some people hire attorneys and sue the federal government. Thus, the lawyers' employment depends on a federal program. Of course, the government may employ investigators and lawyers to investigate the claimants and prove they are not disabled.

> **Example 4:** Overly complicated tax codes have given rise to software companies, tax preparers, and accountants, who help taxpayers remain compliant. Consequently, these professionals would be unemployed if the federal and state governments simplified the tax codes.

> ➢ **Example 5:** Everyone knows a court case in which a judge or jury awarded large damage awards. People are determined to play the lawsuit lottery. Attorneys do not mind because they get paid, whether they win or lose a case. Furthermore, the judges do not mind because they are working and maintaining full dockets. Then they ask legislators for more funding, hire more judges, and build more courthouses. See how we end up in this vicious cycle?

It is challenging to reform a parasitic class after it becomes a dominant class. When a large group of people depends on the government for their livelihood, they fight against any reform or changes threatening them. For example, if Congress and the President streamlined the tax code and made it simple, several corporations would go bankrupt while thousands of tax preparers, accountants, and tax lawyers become unemployed. If we want proof, look at Greece. Between 2010 and 2012, the Greek government had severe financial problems and reduced its spending. Unions, workers, and people went on strikes and protests. Several protests erupted into violence as protestors clashed with the police. Some Americans believe Greece is a prelude to what will happen in the United States within several years.

Conclusion

Judges in courts today differ from judges from a century ago. During the 19th century, judges were pro-business. For example, citizens could file a nuisance lawsuit against a factory because factories generate pollution and noise. However, the citizens usually lost their court cases because judges knew the factories employed workers and created wealth.

Contemporary judges differ from the judges in the 19th century. Businesses and law-abiding citizens usually lose court cases, even for frivolous matters. Unfortunately, people and managers do not have perfect foresight and do not know the infinite ways for idiots to abuse their products. Several silly lawsuits include:

> **Lawsuit 1:** Two people mowing their lawn had a bright idea. They picked up a running lawnmower to hedge bushes. Unfortunately, the lawnmower chopped off their fingers. Then the idiots sued the lawnmower company because the company did not provide any warning or disclaimer for using a lawnmower to hedge bushes.

> **Lawsuit 2:** A burglary tried breaking into someone's home by climbing onto the roof. Unfortunately, the burglar fell through the roof, landed on the floor, and was shot by the homeowner. Although the burglar committed a crime, he sued the homeowner for using excessive force [8].

> **Lawsuit 3:** Asbestos led to the largest and most expensive litigation in U.S. history. Construction companies used asbestos as a common building material because it was an excellent fire retardant and insulator. Unfortunately, people who breathe in asbestos fibers can develop respiratory illnesses such as mesothelioma, lung cancer, and asbestosis. Consequently, lawyers sued the asbestos industry, and the industry started a fund to pay future asbestos claims. Unfortunately, everybody likes to play the lawsuit lottery. People who thought they saw asbestos sued for a piece of pie because they felt they could develop an illness. The industry has not used asbestos since the 1980s, but in 2002, more than 8,400 defendants and 730,000 claimants sued or plan to sue the industry [9].

The English standard law system is excellent but depends on good judges. Good judges can help rein in the legal system, stopping out-of-control attorneys and zealous prosecutors. If a judge truly believes in truth, justice, and the law, they uncover the truth and ensure justice. Judges punish the guilty and set the innocent free. However, if a judge does not want to appear weak on crime or appear politically incorrect, then the judge sweeps the truth and justice under the rug.

References

[1] Savage, David G. October 22, 2008. "Roe vs. Wade? Bush vs. Gore? What are the worst Supreme Court decisions?" *Los Angeles Times*, Available at http://www.latimes.com/news/nationworld/nation/la-na-scotus23-2008oct23,0,1693757.story (access date 12/12/08).

[2] U.S. Supreme Court. 2006. "Massachusetts et al. v. Environmental Protection Agency et al." Available at http://www.supremecourtus.gov/opinions/06pdf/05-1120.pdf (01/03/09).

[3] Sherman, Stratford P. March 17, 1986. "The Man Who Got Hit for $10.5 Billion." *CNN Money*. Available at http://money.cnn.com/magazines/fortune/fortune_archive/1986/03/17/67302/index.htm (access date: 01/03/09).

[4] Attkisson, Sharyl. April 2, 2004. "High Cost of Malpractice Insurance." *CBS Broadcasting, Inc.*

[5] Wikipedia. May 2008. "Liebeck v. McDonald's Restaurants." Available at www.wikipedia.org (access date 5/10/08).

[6] Associated Press. May 3, 2007. "Judge: Cleaner owes me $65 million for pants - 2 years of litigation x 1 pair of trousers = headaches for family business." *MSNBC*.

[7] Associated Press. April 13, 2005. "Finger-in-chili accuser has litigious history." *MSNBC*.

[8] *Channel 3000*. September 21, 2006. "Accused Burglar Sues Homeowner Who Shot Him." Available at http://www.channel3000.com/news/9905807/detail.html?rss=c3k&psp=news (access date 01/03/09).

[9] Wikipedia. December 2008. "Asbestos." Available at www.wikipedia.org (access date 12/31/08).

4. Excessive Regulations

"If we had to follow all the regulations, then Russia would not be growing at 7%."

-A Russian Businessman

A regulation is when the government limits the behavior of individuals or businesses because it sees a problem in society and wants to correct it. The only way for the government to know whether people follow a regulation is to expand a regulatory agency or establish a new one that enforces the limitation.

Regulations are not necessarily harmful! Some regulations make society better off. Several examples of reasonable regulations include the following:

> The government established the U.S. Department of Agriculture to inspect food and to reduce contaminated foods from entering the food supply.

> The U.S. Government established the Federal Aviation Administration to regulate airspace and inspect airplanes.

> The government founded the Federal Trade Commission to investigate monopolies. Thus, the federal government could regulate or break up a monopoly.

A monopoly is a firm that controls a market or a product. Thus, by definition, a monopoly does not have competition. Then the monopolist reduces production, raising the market price and earning enormous profits. Monopolies usually form in the petroleum, communications, electricity, and natural gas industries.

A government regulates the market, curbing a monopolist's power. This is why corporate mergers require permission from the government; mergers allow companies to expand into larger ones as they acquire smaller companies. Growing companies can grow into monopolies.

Government implementing regulations is a complex process involving politicians, interest groups, industries, and regulatory agencies. Furthermore, various groups strive to control or influence regulatory agencies and politicians. Interest groups can form for any purpose or cause. Common interest groups include the following:

➢ Consumers want low prices and safe products.

➢ Stores want access to cheap Chinese imports.

➢ Manufacturing wants to earn high, stable profits, so it wants the government to restrict international trade and labor unions.

➢ Labor unions strive for higher workers' wages, thus reducing businesses' profits and raising business costs.

The fastest method to gain control over the regulatory agency is for interest groups to capture the politicians who control the law-making process. Campaign contributions become the sure, quick, and easy method because politicians want to remain in office, but political campaigns cost millions. For example, the campaign cost to win a House seat in Congress averaged $1 million in 2004, while a Senate seat cost $7 million. Unfortunately, the person with the most money wins. Hence, politicians beg and solicit interest groups for money by knocking on people's doors or using mail, the internet, and the telephone [1, 2].

Campaign contributions can influence politicians' decisions. If a company contributes $1 million to a politician's campaign, and this company wants a particular law, the politician will help him. Once politicians win and get into office, they always set their eyes on the next election or a higher position in government. They need a continuous flow of campaign contributions to help sponsor them. Politicians must find real jobs and work for wages if they lose elections. Remember that old joke, "Talking to politicians is fine, but with a little money, politicians hear us better."

One problem is that a large portion of campaign contributions flow to consultants. During the 2003-2004 federal elections, consultants earned almost $2 billion. For example, President Bush paid $177 million to Maverick Media for his 2004 election commercials [2]. The problem is that the consultants inform politicians how to win the election, such as which issues to side with, which interest groups to ask for money, and which laws and regulations to propose.

Politicians and consultants want to win the election at any cost. Once in office, they focus on the next election and the ensuing fundraising round. Thus, politicians do not pass laws and regulations to make society better off; their goal is to get into office, support any issues that get them there, garner campaign contributions, and pass any laws that make their interest groups happy. Consequently, politicians are career politicians who cater to special interest groups.

Educated people also exacerbate the expansion of regulations because they use rules to generate business for their specialties. Unfortunately, a complicated, convoluted regulatory system boosts demand for professionals. Several examples include the following:

> **Example 1:** Certified Public Accountants (CPAs) want an overly complicated tax code. Thus, businesses and people hire them to ensure that they comply with the tax rules and pay the lowest level of taxes. If the United States passed a simple, flat-income tax, most CPAs would be standing in the unemployment line.

> **Example 2:** Counselors want everyone to get counseling. Any minor cases brought before a criminal court judge usually require counseling. Counselors aid truant kids, married couples, alcoholics, and drug addicts. Unfortunately, this counseling is not free, and the evidence is unclear whether counseling helps people. With all the violence and wars that plagued humanity, we somehow made it to the 20th century without psychologists and counselors. Remember, Sigmund Freud invented psychology and counseling in the 1880s; incidentally, three-quarters of his patients were wealthy.

> **Example 3:** Universities and colleges want education to be a continuous process. Many occupational licenses from state governments, such as teaching certifications, CPAs, etc., require people to continually take courses for their annual re-certification. These courses are available through the internet and cost several hundred dollars.

Politicians, consultants, and educated people help expand government regulations to the point where regulations are out of control. During the last 40 years, social regulations have exploded in the United States. A social regulation means a government regulates behavior that makes society better off, which can be anything. For example, during the mid-1960s and 1970s, the U.S. government established the following agencies:

> **The Environmental Protection Agency** (EPA) helps to decrease pollution and improve the environment.

> **The Occupational Safety and Health Administration** (OSHA) helps improve worker safety standards. OSHA can dictate which machines and equipment employers can use to satisfy regulations.

> **The Equal Employment Opportunity Commission** (EEOC) ensures employers do not discriminate against minorities and women for job hiring, promotions, or working conditions.

> **The Consumer Product Safety Commission** (CPSC) ensures safe consumer products. CPSC can force businesses to recall consumer products if the CPSC believes products are not secure.

> **The Federal Emergency Management Agency** (FEMA) helps local communities devastated by a natural disaster such as an earthquake or hurricane. FEMA provides food, medicine, and shelter to needy residents.

The government created these agencies to improve society. For instance, the EPA must reduce pollution and the harm pollutants cause to the public. However, the EPA dictates its goals and tells industry which equipment to buy to reduce pollution. A business has no say about the costs.

A better approach uses a market, where the government tells the industry how much to reduce pollution. The industry decides how to meet these goals. EPA has implemented some market incentives for sulfur dioxide and mercury pollution emissions.

Another problem is the bureaucracies become incompetent, or the regulations become complex, silly, and onerous. Several examples include the following:

➤ **Example 1:** OHSA specified the height of handrails and the spacing of posts in a workplace.

➤ **Example 2:** Churches, thrift stores, or people sell second-hand goods at garage sales, flea markets, or through the internet. People cannot sell one of the thousands of products the CPSC recalled. CPSC started Resale Roundup, where enforcement officers searched vigorously for violators on the internet. They track down, arrest, and jail anyone who resells an item appearing on the CPSC recall list [3]. Unfortunately, safety standards have no bounds, and neither does stupidity.

➤ **Example 3:** FEMA tends to be slow and bureaucratic and hampers rescue efforts. It showed poor leadership during Hurricanes Hugo in 1989, Andrew in 1992, and Katrina in 2005. In its defense, FEMA tends to be poorly funded and a dumping ground for politically connected appointees with no experience [4].

➤ **Example 4:** The Texas Workforce Commission forces yoga training schools and studios to apply for a certificate or request an exemption. The state can fine the studios and schools $50,000 for non-compliance, while a certificate can cost between $1,000 and $3,000 annually. Since Texas does not have an income tax, the state agencies aggressively collect fees and fines. Some yoga studios closed down, while others banded together to challenge the state [5]. Sometimes, we must ask why the state is so petty and inconsequential.

- ➢ **Example 5:** People can legally buy cigarettes in the U.S. if they are 18 or older. However, state governments heavily taxed cigarettes, won multimillion-dollar lawsuits against tobacco companies in the 1990s, and passed many laws restricting tobacco use. Many state and city governments ban cigarette smoking in restaurants, bars, building entrances, schools, children, cars, etc. Instead of having thousands of these regulations, it would be simpler to make tobacco illegal. Of course, if smoking were prohibited, then the government could not collect money from lawsuits and high cigarette taxes.

- ➢ **Example 6:** Criminal sentencing rules are so complicated in Texas that judges, prosecutors, and prison officials cannot figure them out. Consequently, prisoners hire attorneys and sue the state to determine their remaining prison time. Then compound this problem with inmate overcrowding, budget problems, and parole hearings [6]. This is very foolish because a jury or judge determines the time for a convicted felon. Then the state grants a parole board the power to release nonviolent criminals early to relieve overcrowding. If the state imposed simple, straightforward rules, then Texas would not have this problem. Remember – complicated regulations create a demand for more professionals such as attorneys.

These glaring examples indicate regulations are out of control in the United States. For example, the Office of Advocacy—a small office within the U.S. federal government—estimated that a small business spent $7,647 per employee in 2005 to comply with federal regulations, while a large business spent $5,282. A small business employs fewer than 20 employees, while a large one employs more than 500 [7].

Although small businesses create most jobs, the government imposes a large share of the regulatory burden upon them. Some claim large corporations love regulations because they reduce competition and prevent small businesses from growing into large ones. Then the large corporations can contribute campaign contributions to politicians, who pass favorable laws for the corporations.

Parkinson's Laws

C. Northcote Parkinson observed regulatory agencies expand in size each year without any relationship to the amount of work they do, which became Parkinson's Law. Northcote noticed that as the British Empire shrank, the number of employees in the Colonial Office increased. The Colonial Office administered the British Empire, and a smaller empire implies less work [8, 9]. Thus, the number of employees should decrease over time and not increase!

Parkinson's Law, a universal principle, applies to all government agencies. As Parkinson observed, the total number of employees within a bureaucracy tends to rise by 5-7% per year, regardless of any variation in the amount of work to be done [8,9]. This inevitability is explained by Northcote through three key statements.

> **Statement 1:** "Expenditures rise to meet income." An agency always spends its funding, regardless of funding level. Legislators will notice if a government agency saves money, which could reduce future financing. Moreover, government bureaucrats always request additional funding and then spend it [8, 9].

> **Statement 2:** "Work expands to fill the time available for its completion." If a bureaucrat needs four hours to complete a task and has an 8-hour workday, the bureaucrat will expand

the task into eight hours. Thus, the bureaucrats must create work [8, 9], whether creating new forms or forcing citizens to jump through new hoops for permits, approvals, or other documents.

> **Statement 3:** Bureaucrats will "multiply subordinates, not rivals." Suppose a bureaucrat hires a rival, and that rival competes for the same promotions. However, bureaucrats can elevate themselves to managers by hiring subordinates. To hire subordinates, bureaucrats must "create work for each other" [8, 9].

Bureaucrats, driven by self-interest and the desire for job security, design long-term programs and continually expand the size, scope, and mission of government. Over time, regulatory agencies expand paperwork, broaden regulations, and increase complexity. Educated bureaucrats, aware that complex rules can lead to higher salaries and increased demand for their services, actively seek to create and maintain such complexity. This self-interest is a key factor in the continual expansion, rather than contraction, of bureaucracies.

The Government, Technology, and Urbanization

Technology encourages the growth and intrusiveness of government bureaucracies. As technology improves for communication, transportation, and record keeping, bureaucracies become larger. Bureaucrats use technology to enhance monitoring and ensure compliance with their rules and regulations [10].

For example, smugglers secretly import products and avoid paying duties and taxes to the government. The government uses several methods to combat this. First, customs agents use planes, ships, radar, and satellites to track down boats and airplanes, not docking them at the ports. This vast network searches the skies and seas for violators and smugglers. Second, if the smugglers successfully get their products to the stores and merchants, government agents can backtrack and trace them back to the smugglers. Stores and merchants record their transactions on documents that government agents can scrutinize. Records allow government agents to match what a merchant sells to his purchases. If a merchant claims he bought all his merchandise from one distributor, the agents can check that distributor's records for discrepancies. Finally, tax agents will investigate anyone who carries too much cash and cannot explain where the money came from.

One hundred years ago, government did not have this technology. Consequently, the government had difficulties tracking down and prosecuting smugglers. Thus, the United States maintained a capitalistic and market-oriented economy.

The national government uses technology to dominate the entire economy and uses bureaucracies to control cities, villages, and communities far from the bureaucracies [10].

The government maintains large computer databases of people and businesses. If government agents think someone has violated a rule or regulation, they can have a team of agents there within hours, using planes, helicopters, or cars. It is no coincidence that the U.S. government has usurped power away from the states. Consequently, bureaucrats in Washington, D.C., are bombarding the county and city governments with numerous rules and regulations. Thus, technology expands the intrusiveness of government.

For example, a business opens an illegal mine in the backwoods of Montana. Eventually, the bureaucrats in Washington, D.C., hear about the mine and have agents and regulators there within hours to investigate. The mine will show up on a satellite image, or an angry environmentalist will report the mine to the government. One hundred years ago, this mine could operate in secrecy without being caught. The government was too far and remote to intervene in a business's affairs.

Drug testing is another example of intrusiveness and has become a recent phenomenon. Employers and the government could not do drug testing before the 1990s. Judges, government officials, high-school principals, and employers want drug testing, even for low-paying jobs.

Drug testing is biased towards only one drug – marijuana. If a person smokes a joint, the active ingredient, tetrahydracannibal (THC), remains in the fatty tissues of the body for a month or more. On the other hand, if people use cocaine, meth, amphetamines, or barbiturates, they abstain from those drugs for two days, and their urine will test clean because the human body quickly metabolizes these drugs.

Many U.S. institutions are intrusive and want drug testing for a wide range of people. Of course, drug-testing companies profit significantly from this expanding industry. In 2011, the governors of Michigan and Florida wanted all state employees tested for illegal drugs. Incidentally, the governors indirectly own the medical clinics that would do the testing.

Before the 1990s, an employer checking criminal records would go to the local courthouse and search the court records. Of course, employers only checked for crimes committed in their county, and convicted felons could move to a new county or across a state line, starting a new life. Criminal records did not follow people in the old days.

Since the 1990s, the government and large companies created massive computer databases. Consequently, a criminal record can trail after a person like shackles anywhere within a country. A criminal record exists forever and never goes away. Databases' dominion grows at an alarming rate. Within several years, criminal records will follow a person across countries. Unfortunately, the U.S. criminal system evolved into a puritanical one without forgiveness. People can have their lives destroyed over a minor incident. For example, the unemployment situation has become so bad in 2012 that an employer will not hire any employee if anything negative comes up. That trespassing charge or drunken driving incident from college can haunt a person for the rest of their lives.

Companies report customer information to credit bureaus, such as ChexSystems, Experian, TransUnion, and Equifax. In theory, banks and companies report their customers' creditworthiness. Nevertheless, they use these credit bureaus as a stick to beat on their customers' heads.

For example, if a customer overdrafts their checking account, the bank adds exorbitant fees to the account. In the old days, a customer could walk away and not pay the outrageous fees. Now, the customer must pay these fees, even if an overdraft results in hundreds of dollars in penalties. The banks report outstanding balances to ChexSystems. Subsequently, that person cannot open another bank account until they pay the fees.

In some cases, banks delay payments or apply withdrawals before credits, which boosts the chance of an overdraft. Consequently, banks collude with each other via ChexSystems, like the mafia, to extract as much profits as they can from their customers. Unfortunately, employers want access to a person's credit history, even for jobs where good credit is not necessary for job performance.

Satellites in the sky form the backbone of a GPS. A GPS device receives a radio signal from the satellites and calculates the device's location within inches, anywhere on the earth's surface. Unfortunately, GPS has opened new avenues of surveillance. Federal agents can track people of interest with GPS monitoring devices, usually connected to a person's car, even without a court order.

Imagine two agents physically following a suspect around in the old days. Agencies expended manpower to survey a person. Currently, those two agents can track thousands of suspects with GPS as agents sit behind a computer screen and track people without leaving the office. Modern cars automatically come with a GPS. Thus, the agents do not expend energy to install a GPS on a car because manufacturers have already installed them in modern vehicles.

The government could track people once the GPS devices become small enough to be implanted into the human body. First, the government will require felons to get GPS implants, then anyone convicted of misdemeanors. Next, anyone viewed as a threat to the government will require implants. Finally, the government will recommend parents get GPS implants for kids so they can be located quickly if kidnappers grab their children. Of course, the government will never remove these implants. Thus, everyone will have GPS implants, and the government will monitor everyone. Then the U.S. government evolves into a totalitarian state.

Government agents can track cell phones, but GPS is more accurate. Some state governments are cracking down on pre-paid cell phones because the user remains anonymous. The government wants a person's identity tied to his cell phone.

Modern vehicles contain a black box, which is a computer. The computer adjusts the car's engine and transmission to reduce pollution. However, the computer remembers. As we guessed, attorneys file paperwork with the court to grab their sticky hands on those black boxes. Those black boxes remember how fast people drove before the accident or whether the driver hit the brakes. Black boxes open new avenues for government.

Some legislators are debating laws requiring a car's computer to include Global Position Satellites (GPS). GPS tracks a car's location anywhere on the earth's surface. Then a state government monitors a driver's mileage and sends the driver a tax bill to repair and maintain highways and roads. Why stop there? A car's computer, connected to a GPS, can keep track of a driver's speed. Thus, if the driver speeds, the computer communicates this information to the local police, where a computer system automatically issues a speeding citation.

Although the government can use technology with good intentions, sometimes politicians and bureaucrats go too far. For example, all states have laws requiring sex offenders to register with the police. The police then enter this information into a sex-offender database that the public can access freely.

The government is not wrong to establish these databases. However, these databases create two problems. First, a court does not list an offender's specific crimes or at least not in detail. For example, a court convicted an 18-year-old boy of statutory rape of his 17-year-old girlfriend even if they both attended the same grade in high school. He must register as a sex offender. Second, legislators and police are expanding the list of offenses that require offenders to register, even for non-sexual crimes. The reason some crimes endanger the public. Thus, offenders must register because they are endangering the public. Is any crime a safety concern for the public? For instance, a person who speeds threatens the public. Hence, should speeders register as sex offenders because their speeding threatens public safety?

Urbanization creates another factor that expands and enlarges a government's intrusiveness. People living in the country migrate to the cities, searching for work and escaping the misery and poverty of rural communities. Unfortunately, urbanization always leads to a larger government and more bureaucracies.

Imagine living in a rural community and raising cattle. Which services can the government provide? Ranchers are self-sufficient and require little government services because wide-open spaces separate them.

Cities have a greater population density as thousands live close to each other. This closeness sparks conflict and problems. For instance, urban areas consume large quantities of fresh water and generate large amounts of garbage, wastewater, and pollution, which stress the environment. Finally, crime, noise, and traffic congestion plague large cities. Consequently, local government expands to reduce these problems, and urban dwellers pay higher taxes than people living in the suburbs or the country.

City governments impose stronger regulations, higher taxes, and more building codes than rural communities. Rich and middle-class residents become tired of an intrusive city government and poor government services, so they migrate to the suburbs. As the city loses tax revenue and citizens, it annexes the surrounding suburbs, expanding and enlarging a more bureaucratic government.

The Problems of Regulations

The government is a unique institution. Regulatory agencies can waste taxpayer money, and then the government turns around and raises taxes and fees to cover any budget shortfalls. No other institution in our society has that power. Two examples hone this point:

> ➤ **Example 1:** The U.S. government passed the Nuclear Waste Policy Act to locate a disposal spot for the nation's nuclear

waste. The government founded and developed a geographically stable site in Yucca Mountain, Nevada, that sits next to the atomic weapons test site. The government bored a 5-mile-long U-shaped tunnel into the mountain. However, political opposition and lawsuits delayed the opening of this facility for decades. Meanwhile, the U.S. military and nuclear electric power plants are stockpiling atomic waste at their facilities. As of 2008, the government has wasted approximately $9 billion on this project.

➤ **Example 2:** The Federal Emergency Management Agency (FEMA) had 10,770 vacant trailers at a deserted military airport in rural Hope, Arkansas. FEMA stockpiled trailers as temporary housing for victims of natural disasters. Unfortunately, FEMA did not make trailers available to Hurricane Katrina victims because federal law prohibits trailers from being used in a flood plain. Instead, victims and survivors were living in tents. The government paid $431 million for these vacant trailers [11].

Regulatory agencies may produce the opposite impact than intended. For example, the federal government passed laws and regulations to protect historic buildings and sites. On the surface, this appears to be a good law because the government protects history. However, these regulations destroy landmark homes.

Suppose a nonprofit or contractor rehabilitates a historic home using government funds and then sells it to a family. Subsequently, the agency encounters three problems.

➤ **Problem 1:** A nonprofit or contractor applies for permits (or permission) from a historic government agency. Historic bureaucrats can take a long time to approve and subject the project to their whim. If the authority is a state government agency, receiving a response takes six months or more. Thus, historic preservation agencies add another level of bureaucracy.

> **Problem 2:** Historic preservation raises the rehabilitation costs. For instance, if the house needs new windows, a contractor cannot simply rip out the old windows and install new ones. This destroys the "historic integrity" of the home. Instead, the person must repair each window to match the original design, which could significantly increase the rehabilitation cost.

> **Problem 3:** Homebuyers are not interested in buying historic homes because ownership has many restrictions. Homeowners need permission from a government agency like Historic Preservation to paint, renovate, or install new equipment, such as an air conditioner in historic homes.

Consequently, nonprofits and developers avoid historic houses because they must deal with the historic preservation bureaucracy, are more expensive to rehabilitate, and are more difficult to sell. Therefore, these homes sit vacant until the government bulldozes them when they become a hazard to the community. Consequently, historic preservation regulations encouraged the destruction of historic homes.

Other problems of regulations include the following:

> **Problem 1:** Federal, state, and county governments pass regulations that could conflict with each other. For example, the State of California legalized marijuana for medicinal purposes while the U.S. federal government still considers any marijuana use illegal. For another example, the U.S. Department of Energy wanted electric power plants to use more coal during the 1970s to reduce the reliance on imported petroleum. However, the U.S. Environmental Protection Agency penalized coal use because it is a dirty fuel [12].

> **Problem 2:** Regulations become rigid as bureaucrats become used to regulating in a particular manner. They rarely change as society changes.

➢ **Problem 3:** Bureaucrats are more concerned with maintaining their jobs and importance than helping people. They become skilled at justifying their programs and importance to legislators because legislatures allocate funding and money.

➢ **Problem 4:** Different government workers interpret the laws and regulations differently. Some government workers are strict, while others are lax. For example, Internal Revenue Service (IRS) workers give conflicting information to taxpayers because tax laws are too complex, and everyone interprets them differently.

➢ **Problem 5:** People with agendas and hidden motives may penetrate and become leaders of government bureaucracies. For example, an environmentalist who hates corporations becomes the director of an environmental agency, creating red tape and problems for businesses. A woman who hates men becomes a judge or prosecutor for a domestic violence court or a family court. Consequently, any man brought to court must be found guilty.

➢ **Problem 6:** Large corporations prefer more complicated regulations because regulations create an entry market barrier. For instance, if rules are demanding and complex, potential new competitors cannot enter the market. A large corporation can absorb these costs by creating a specialized department that keeps the corporation in compliance with the regulations. Unfortunately, small companies cannot afford this small department of professionals.

➢ **Problem 7:** Regulatory agencies and their regulated companies become "too friendly" over time. Thus, regulators may become lenient on their regulated companies. Corruption represents an extreme form of "too friendly" as company managers pay bribes to regulators. High-ranking government officials often become consultants and work for the companies they once regulated.

Society's Costs of Regulations

Regulations create a demand for bureaucrats, and bureaucracies consume financial resources. They depend on fees, fines, and taxes to finance their budgets. Thus, every time the government establishes a new bureaucracy or expands an old one, the government needs more funding. The total costs of a bureaucracy include the following:

> **Cost 1:** Bureaucracies raise businesses' costs. Bureaucracies regulate and enforce the law, which imposes enforcement costs and regulatory burdens on the private sector. Consequently, enterprises submit documents to the government, invest in new equipment, and hire compliance specialists.

> **Cost 2:** The government diverts resources from the private sector to the regulatory agency. The government pays bureaucrats' salaries by collecting taxes, fines, and fees, shifting resources from the private sector to the public. Thus, salaries comprise the largest item in regulatory agencies' budgets. If the government did not employ staff, they would work in the private markets.

> **Cost 3:** Taxes and regulations have a profound impact on economic activity, potentially disrupting the market. The financing of regulatory agencies through taxes, and the expansion of tax authorities, adds another layer of bureaucracy that consumes resources. Moreover, taxes always lead to increased prices and reduced market quantities, as consumers cut back on spending when products become more expensive, thereby affecting the overall economic activity.

> **Cost 4:** Taxes and regulations create violators. When the government makes regulations or imposes taxes, some people will violate the regulations or evade taxes. Consequently, the government consumes resources to enforce and punish violators. The government must expand its courts and prison systems.

As the government establishes more bureaucracies, which grow larger relative to the economy, they slow economic growth and stifle free enterprise. A declining economy generates less wealth and lowers the tax base, leading to a vicious cycle of increasing taxes, fines, and regulations to offset declining tax revenue. This cycle, in turn, leads to a stagnating and decaying society.

Conclusion

The United States has undergone three significant growth spurts, each necessitating the creation of many regulatory institutions. These growth spurts show the crucial role of regulatory agencies in shaping the nation's economic and social institutions.

> **Regulating Industry:** From 1870 to 1910, the government's establishment of new institutions and expansion of power impacted the economy. The federal government's inspection of food, breakup of monopolies, and regulation of railroad rates, along with state governments' imposition of price controls and creation of public service commissions, all contributed to a more regulated economy.

> **Government Expands the Economy:** Franklin Roosevelt established numerous new institutions during the Great Depression, which lasted from 1929 to 1940. Roosevelt tried to get the U.S. economy to grow again by stabilizing the financial markets, imposing price and wage controls, and creating the first national pension fund, Social Security.

> **The Growth of Social Regulations:** From the 1970s to the present, government at all levels has imposed its beliefs onto society. Thus, all governments have increased their regulatory powers over everything concerning private property, families, businesses, and industries.

The establishment of new regulatory institutions also presents a challenge. These institutions, once created, rarely disappear. Instead, they adapt and evolve, broadening their influence and altering their mission to meet the changing needs of society.

For example, President Roosevelt founded the Tennessee Valley Authority (TVA) in 1933, which helped modernize Tennessee and provided electricity to rural areas. TVA has met its mission, but it still lives. Currently, TVA subsidizes electricity to households.

Some regulatory agencies never achieve their objectives. For instance, the U.S. government established the Department of Energy (DOE) in 1977 because of the oil crisis of 1973, when Arab nations stopped shipping petroleum to the United States. The oil embargo sparked a supply shock to the U.S. economy, leading to a recession. Accordingly, the DOE's objective was to reduce the United States' reliance on imported petroleum. In 1973, the U.S. imported 2.2 billion barrels of oil, which rose to 3.1 billion barrels in 2011. Consequently, the DOE has failed its mission.

The U.S. government founded the Department of Urban Development (HUD) in 1965 to provide affordable housing and rental units, protect consumers, and improve the quality of life. However, urban blight and low-quality housing remain problems in large cities, and thus, this agency failed miserably.

The government sometimes creates agencies that society does not need. For example, President Roosevelt started the excise tax on gasoline to finance highway construction without a government department. Then President Eisenhower began constructing the interstate highway system that linked the major cities between states during the 1950s. Finally, the U.S. government established the Department of Transportation (DOT) in 1967 to create a fast, efficient, and safe transportation system.

References

[1] Becker, Gary S. 1983. "A Theory of Competition among Pressure Groups for Political Influence." *The Quarterly Journal of Economics*. 98(3): 371-400.

[2] Bergo, Sandy. September 26, 2006. "A Wealth of Advice - Nearly $2 billion flowed through consultants in 2003-2004 federal elections." *The Center of Public Integrity*.

[3] Rosen, James. August 20, 2009. "Seller, beware: Feds cracking down on secondhand sales of some products." *Kansas City Star*.

[4] McQuaid, John and Mark Schleifstein. 2006. *Path of Destruction*. New York: Little Brown and Company, pp. 112-114, pp. 308-344.

[5] Dulai, Shaminder. August 22, 2010. "Yoga professionals to state: Leave us in peace." *Houston Chronicle*.

[6] Marshall, Thom. November 16, 2003 "Figuring felon prison time growing business for firm." *Houston Chronicle*.

[7] Office of Advocacy. September 19, 2005. "Small Business Hard Hit By Federal Regulatory Compliance Burden." Washington, DC: U.S. Small Business Administration. Available at http://www.sba.gov/advo/press/05-43.html (Access date: 7/11/08).

[8] Parkinson, C. Northcote. 1957. *Parkinson's Law*. Cambridge and Massachusetts: The Riverside Press.

[9] Parkinson, C. Northcote. November 1955. "Parkinson's Law." *The Economist*.

[10] Kiser, Edgar and Joshua Kane. 2001. "Revolution and State Structure: The Bureaucratization of Tax Administration in Early Modern England and France." *The American Journal of Sociology* 107(1): 183-223

[11] Neuman, Johanna. February 10, 2006. "The Land of 10,770 Empty FEMA Trailers." *The Los Angeles Times*.

[12] Palmer, Jay. November 27, 1978. "The Rising Risks of Regulation." *Time*.

5. Taxes Destroy Wealth

"People do not work, consume, or invest to pay taxes."

-Arthur B. Laffer

We need a government for a well-functioning economy. For a capitalistic country to thrive, the government must finance three activities: the legal system, national defense, and commerce. These three activities come straight from Adam Smith's *An Inquiry into the Nature and Causes of the Wealth of Nations*.

> **Activity 1:** The government establishes a legal system or game rules. A government with an excellent legal system helps protect private property rights, enforce contracts, and settle disputes. Hence, the government establishes police, fire departments, and various courts to administer "justice." Consequently, any legal system with substantial property rights will have wealthy property owners that the government will defend at the expense of the poor.

> **Activity 2:** The government protects its interests, people, and land from invading armies, navies, and aircraft. Thus, the government finances a military.

> **Activity 3:** The government encourages commerce. Hence, the government invests in infrastructure such as bridges, highways, harbors, canals, and airports. Good infrastructure connects people and markets together. Then regions within a nation specialize as they transport their goods quickly to markets anywhere around the country and the world. Finally, the government coins money that people and businesses use in commerce.

Private companies could carry out the functions of government. However, these institutions would possess enormous powers, and the public may develop an intense hatred for them and shun them. For example, would we trust a person to own and manage a police or fire department? For instance, Marcus Licinus Crassus owned the first fire department in Rome. Crassus negotiated the price for his services as a person's house was burning down. Usually, Crassus bought the property at a discount and added it to his wealth.

Many experts and philosophers in the 18th century added another critical function to government—education. An educated workforce develops technical skills, transforming an agricultural society into an industrial one. This argument is still around today—just change technical skills to computer skills. These economists said the government should promote education, which does not mean micro-managing it. Consequently, all countries created an education system that includes schools, colleges, and universities.

People and political leaders have added many functions to government. Consequently, governments provide a network of parks and reserves, construct and manage libraries, deliver mail, protect the environment, and reduce income inequality. Thus, pursuing a Utopian society has expanded the government's size, scope, and mission.

For the government to provide its critical functions to society, it must collect taxes to pay for them. Economists define a tax system as the ratio between a household's taxes and income, classifying it into three types: progressive, proportional, and regressive.

A progressive tax rate is one in which the average tax rate rises with income. For instance, the income taxes in the United States are progressive. Low-income households pay small average tax rates, while high-income households pay higher tax rates. In 2005, the top 5 percent of wage earnings paid an average tax rate of 20.8%, while the bottom 50 percent paid an average tax rate of 3%. Many believe this tax system is fair because the "rich" are stuck with higher tax burdens.

A proportional tax rate is the average tax rate that stays the same across all income levels. For example, Russia and the Republic of Kazakhstan impose flat income tax rates of 13% and 11%, respectively. Thus, the rich and poor pay the government the same proportion of their income.

A proportional tax system has two excellent properties. First, taxpayers do not remit taxes to the government. Workers' employers automatically withhold and remit taxes to the government. Only the employers submit paperwork to the government. Second, businesses and people can predict future tax payments. For each dollar a person makes, they know the percentage that goes to the government. Hence, a proportional tax system would be the simplest and the easiest to administer and enforce.

A proportional tax system has one significant problem. Businesses can employ workers illegally. Employers can remit taxes to the government for illegal workers by using tax IDs from legitimate workers. Legitimate workers may never find out because they never verify their income with the government.

A regressive tax rate is the average tax rate that falls as a person's income increases. For example, a sales tax on food constitutes a regressive tax. If two families spend $10,000 each on food annually and the sales tax rate equals 10%, the government collects $1,000 from each family. If the first family earns $50,000 in income, their average food tax rate equals 2%. If a second family has an income of $10,000, then they pay a 10% tax on their food. Thus, the tax hits low-income families harder.

The government imposes various regressive taxes. The U.S. government funds Social Security and Medicare through regressive taxes. The federal government stops collecting Medicare and Social Security taxes once income exceeds $110,100 annually. Property, excise, and sales taxes are also regressive because the government does not use income to determine tax rates. Thus, these taxes hit the poor much more than the rich. Moreover, governments impose excise taxes on alcohol, tobacco, and gasoline. An excise tax is a tax on a specific good for a particular amount, while a sales tax is a percentage applied to a product's value that applies to a broad class of goods sold in stores and shops.

The tax code in the United States is difficult to analyze because it is riddled with numerous exemptions and tax credits. A common rumor is that the U.S. tax code is so complex that members of Congress hire accountants to calculate and file their tax returns. Ironically, these same imbeciles passed these tax laws! If the people who passed these stupid laws cannot understand them, then how can people outside the tax profession understand them?

The U.S. income tax system has three major shortcomings:

> **Shortcoming 1:** Taxpayers have a difficult time determining their true tax burden. If families experience significant changes in income or situations, they cannot predict how their taxes will change, given all the exceptions and forms.

> **Shortcoming 2:** Taxpayers may not claim all tax credits that reduce their tax burden. For example, some taxpayers fear applying for tax credits because they believe too many credits will trigger an audit. Furthermore, taxpayers must fill out complicated, confusing forms to claim tax credits. On the other hand, some taxpayers abuse the tax credits. They broadly interpret the rules to reduce their tax burden. Consequently, the U.S. tax system is unfair.

> **Shortcoming 3:** Politicians help propagate complicated tax codes. It is a universal truth – everyone hates paying taxes. However, many U.S. leaders are career politicians who favor expanding government. They hand out the most pork possible to their constituents so the voters will reelect them. Politicians usually pass small taxes on everything to prevent public protests and keep inventing new taxes and fees. Furthermore, some clever politicians made campaign promises to reduce one tax but then raise other taxes to cover the shortfall.

The problem of having numerous small taxes leads to more enormous government bureaucracies because the government creates different bureaucracies to collect and enforce all these distinctive small taxes. Tax inspectors also scrutinize every tax credit or exemption for accuracy and errors. It would be simpler to have one or two tax agencies oversee the collection of all taxes. For example, in some states like Texas, school districts, county governments, and water utility districts have bureaucracies to collect their portion of property taxes.

A consequence of economic decline is government agencies with severe financial troubles will force their citizens and businesses to prepay future tax liabilities. (You think this would be illegal). Essentially, taxpayers prepaying a tax give the government an interest-free loan. For example, Michigan has experienced budget problems since the 2001 Recession. Local governments force Michigan's residents to pay their property taxes this year and the next five months of the following year in advance [1].

The Federal Deposit Insurance Corporation (FDIC) has been experiencing financial problems since the 2008 Financial Crisis. As of November 2009, 120 banks failed, causing the FDIC to lose approximately $28 billion. The FDIC insures bank deposits up to $250,000 per depositor. This insurance is not voluntary because regulators force banks to pay it. With the FDIC experiencing financial hardship, banks must pay future insurance three years in advance [2].

The financial crisis hit the banks hard, and the government hurled further hardship onto them. What would happen if the U.S. economy does not turn around and grow again? How far will the government force its citizens to pay taxes in advance?

Taxes Alter Behavior

Politicians elected into office do not understand the long-term consequences of their actions. When a legislator dreams up a new tax or hikes an old one, the legislator believes the tax will not impact human behavior. For example, the legislature and governor passed a new tax on red cars because they think they cause more accidents. If the state has 100 million red vehicles, the tax base will not remain at 100 million. People and businesses can avoid this tax by driving non-red cars. This is a natural phenomenon. If the government sticks its hand into our pocket, we figure a way to keep that hand from grabbing too much money. Furthermore, the court system would be bombarded with lawsuits over the color of red. Is maroon close enough to be considered red and hence taxed?

Political leaders examine their jurisdiction's economic activity and industries, scheming new ways to extract more taxes and fees from their businesses and citizens. For example, state politicians have scrutinized the Internet since the 2008 Financial Crisis.

Many internet businesses do not charge a sales tax for selling items to customers living in other states. Some states have become aggressive towards large internet companies, such as Amazon. State governments want access to customers' records and business transactions, although Amazon may be outside that state. Moreover, some states went after their Indian tribes. Although Indian reservations retain their sovereignty, people flock to the Indian reservations to gamble and buy discounted gasoline and cigarettes. States want a piece of their action.

Tax authorities continually expand the scope and nature of taxes. For example, in St. Joseph County, Indiana, the government wants to impose a wheel tax because the wheels wear and tear the roads, and the government wants drivers to pay for them. The wheel tax produces two problems. First, the state collects an excise tax on gasoline and diesel fuel that the government uses to build and maintain highways. Second, the state imposes numerous taxes on vehicles. If we buy a car in Indiana, we pay the sales tax, a tag fee, a title fee, and an emissions-testing fee. Unfortunately, the wheel tax heavily burdens businesses that use semi-trucks. A semi could have from 4 to 10 wheels without a trailer. If the tax includes a trailer, add another four or more wheels. Hence, this tax becomes another cost burden to businesses.

Taxes raise businesses' operating costs. Thus, businesses pass the costs onto customers, reduce profits, or relocate to another state or country with favorable tax codes. The worst-case scenario is for the company to go bankrupt, with the wheel tax being the straw that broke the camel's back. For example, if St. Joseph County imposed a wheel tax on businesses, a business could circumvent the wheel tax by registering its trucks in Mexico and employing cheaper labor. If a company does not operate in Indiana, then that company does not pay a variety of business taxes and does not employ people who would pay income taxes. Therefore, out-of-control taxes produce more unemployment and lower tax revenue collections.

People may migrate to another state or country to reduce their tax burden. For example, the 2008 Financial Crisis hit many states hard, like California. Consequently, politicians want to hike income taxes for the wealthiest Californians. Unfortunately, California is next door to Nevada, which imposes no state income tax. Some millionaires could leave the state if this tax passes, taking their wealth and assets. The rich already pay more taxes than people with low incomes because they pay progressive federal and state income taxes. If the affluent Californians leave the state, California will increase other taxes to cover the lost tax revenue [3].

Hefty and excessive taxes create black markets and lead to smuggling. For example, Michigan imposed the second-largest tax on cigarettes in 1994, which raised the tax from $0.25 per pack to $0.75. (The tax is $2.00 per pack [4]). Unfortunately, Michigan lies next to Indiana, and Indiana imposes one of the lowest taxes on cigarettes. The tax created almost a $0.50 difference per pack in retail price. What do rational consumers do as prices become steep? They search for places where they can find bargains and head south to Indiana to buy their cigarettes.

The Michigan cigarette tax is foolish for four reasons:

- ➢ **Reason 1:** The tax would force some people to stop smoking, which the politicians claim is their reason for hiking the tax. However, if all smokers had stopped smoking, then the government would not collect these taxes anymore. The 2008 Financial Crisis hit the states hard. Consequently, politicians hiked cigarette taxes to cover the lower tax revenue collections.

- ➢ **Reason 2:** People from Michigan will buy fewer cigarettes in Michigan. Instead, they buy them from Indiana [5]. Tax revenue for Michigan falls as people purchase their cigarettes outside of Michigan. Whether or not Michigan gains more cigarette tax revenues depends on the more significant tax per cigarette pack versus the number of cigarettes bought in Michigan. This is the basis for the Laffer Curve discussed in this chapter.

- ➢ **Reason 3:** Criminal groups become involved and smuggle cigarettes. Smugglers could earn large profits when the government artificially makes a $0.50 per pack price difference [5]. Michigan wants to create jobs, so this will help.

> **Reason 4:** This law creates more violators. Thus, Michigan will spend more money tracking, prosecuting, and incarcerating violators who smuggle cigarettes into the state.

A complex tax system creates another problem – large businesses and corporations prefer complicated, incomprehensible tax codes, while small companies cannot afford to hire tax specialists or consult with attorneys. These specialists are expensive. On the other hand, large businesses can absorb these costs by hiring specialists.

Some taxes, like an inheritance tax, destroy small businesses. A small company is a proprietorship and is dissolved when the owner dies. The business's heirs must reorganize or dissolve it, but they must pay the inheritance tax. For instance, the federal inheritance tax forced many small lumber companies out of business because the heirs liquidated the business to pay these taxes.

Politicians and leaders say the inheritance tax prevents the creation of a plutocracy. A plutocracy represents a political system where the wealthy govern and control the government. However, the inheritance tax has a severe flaw. Since corporations can theoretically live forever, they will never pay an inheritance tax. Consequently, corporations garner wealth and bribe politicians with campaign contributions or gifts, such as exotic vacations, scholarships for children, or reduced mortgage payments. We should coin a new word: corpocracy. Corporations indirectly govern the government by controlling the politicians and political leaders. Of course, another good word is kleptocracy. A system of government where politicians and leaders steal everything they can get their hands on.

Our complex tax system has led to the creation of tax reductions. State and local politicians use tax abatements to attract new businesses to their area. New businesses invest in buildings and equipment and hire workers. Moreover, new companies revive blighted neighborhoods and create jobs. However, tax abatements cause four problems.

> **Problem 1:** The government acknowledges the high taxes and temporarily reduces them to create wealth.

> **Problem 2:** Tax abatements penalize businesses that operate in the community without receiving any tax abatements. Those businesses remaining loyal to their community and paying their taxes suffer a disadvantage. Newcomers enter their market and compete with lower costs from the tax abatement.

> **Problem 3:** Businesses migrate nationwide, searching for communities with the highest tax abatements. After the tax abatement has ended, the business migrates to another community, searching for new tax reductions.

> **Problem 4:** Small businesses do not get these breaks, although small businesses are responsible for most of the job growth in the U.S. economy. Politicians usually wine and dine with large corporations.

The 2008 Financial Crisis added a new twist to tax reductions. Politicians fear further job losses because of the staggering layoffs that occurred in 2009 while the unemployment rate hovers around 10%. Some businesses demanded more tax breaks, or they would close down and relocate to another community, taking the jobs with them. In 2012, the Sears Corporation and the Chicago Board of Trade demanded tax concessions from the State of Illinois, or they would leave the state despite severe financial problems.

The Laffer Curve

The Laffer Curve, a key concept in tax policy, illustrates the intricate relationship between tax rates, tax revenues, and consumer behavior. When the government raises the tax rate, it triggers two opposing effects. On the one hand, the government collects more taxes from each item it taxes. On the other hand, a tax hike invariably leads to higher prices, causing consumers to reduce their consumption. This reduction in consumption takes the form of tax evasion or changes in consumer behavior to mitigate the tax's impact. As a result, a tax increase always leads to a contraction of the tax base [6, 7].

When the government raises a tax, a tax increase has one of these two impacts:

➤ With low tax rates, a government hiking taxes collects more tax revenue. The government collects more revenue from a higher tax rate than the revenue lost from the smaller tax base.

➤ With high tax rates, a government raising taxes collects less tax revenue. Tax base contracts, wiping out the gains from the higher tax rate.

The actual shape of the Laffer Curve, a fundamental concept in economics, remains a mystery. It serves as a valuable teaching tool in economics courses. We know two points on the curve.

➤ The government collects zero tax revenues if the tax rate equals 0%.

➤ If the tax rate is 100%, the government collects zero tax revenue. Nobody will work if the government seizes all their earnings.

The Laffer Curve, which we discussed in Chapter 1, shares similarities with the Rahn Curve. Both curves depict the relationship between tax rates and tax revenues. The Laffer Curve, in particular, takes the shape of an upside-down U, with a specific tax rate that maximizes government revenue. Figure 1 illustrates a Laffer Curve with a 40% tax rate that optimizes tax revenues.

Many bureaucrats and political leaders ignore the Laffer Curve. Leaders always hike taxes and fees to boost tax revenues as the government expands. However, they ignore that high tax rates destroy a market economy and contract the underlying tax base. If politicians see tax revenues fall after a tax increase, they believe people are evading taxes and cheating the government out of its money. Subsequently, these same politicians expand their tax authorities to search for these elusive tax evaders.

Figure 1: An Example of a Laffer Curve

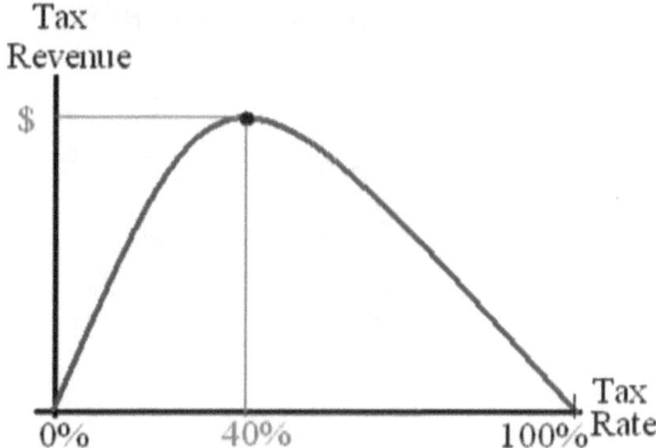

We see the effects of the Laffer Curve on federal excise taxes on gasoline and diesel fuel. Table 1 shows the tax rates and the effective date when the government started collecting the tax. President Roosevelt was the first to impose gasoline taxes and used the tax revenue to construct the U.S. highway system. Moreover, the President used highway construction to create public service jobs during the Great Depression. Table 1 shows two patterns. First, tax rate increases occur more frequently towards the present time. Second, the tax hikes become more significant over time. However, this table does not include the state excise tax, which averages about 6 cents per gallon.

Some people clamor for more taxes on fossil fuels to maintain the highway system and replace dilapidated, crumbling bridges and roads. However, Americans constructed our highway system when taxes were as low as one cent per gallon of gasoline. Unfortunately, the government raising taxes on gasoline and diesel fuel may depress revenues further.

The Laffer Curve was the basis of Reaganomics. President Reagan reduced tax rates during the 1980s as part of his economic plan. Consequently, the U.S. economy grew furiously. Although the average tax rates for the 'rich" fell, the top 1% of income earners paid a whopping 43.9% more in taxes. A flourishing economy always boosts tax revenues, offsetting lower tax rates [7]. Many blame Reagan for the substantial government deficits during the 1980s and the rapid rise in U.S. public debt. However, the U.S. economy had plenty of good-paying jobs with benefits during the 1980s.

Table 1: Federal Excise Taxes on Gasoline and Diesel Fuel

Effective Date	Gasoline (cents per gallon)	Diesel Fuel (cents per gallon)
June 21, 1932	1.0	-
June 17, 1933	1.5	-
January 1, 1934	1.0	-
July 1, 1940	1.5	-
November 1, 1951	2.0	2.0
July 1, 1956	3.0	3.0
October 1, 1959	4.0	4.0
November 10, 1978	4.0	4.0
January 1, 1979	4.0	4.0
April 1, 1983	9.0	9.0
August 1, 1984	9.0	15.0
January 1, 1987	9.1	15.1
December 1, 1990	14.1	20.1
October 1, 1993	18.4	24.4
January 1, 1996	18.3	24.3
October 1, 1997	18.4	24.4

Source: Federal Highway Administration 1999 [8].

Instability in State Government Financing

All state and local governments, except one state, have balanced budget amendments. A balanced budget law should stabilize government finances, but it leads to more instability. This raises the question: Where does this instability originate? The answer lies in politicians' continuous expansion of government, which necessitates increased tax collection, thereby creating financial instability in two key states of the economy.

> **A Growing Economy:** A growing economy lowers unemployment and raises incomes. More people are employed, earn greater incomes, and pay more taxes. Unfortunately, politicians always spend this extra revenue and never save it. They spread the money around, greasing the wheels for their constituents. Thus, politicians constantly expand the government's size.

> **A Recession:** A contracting economy increases unemployment and lowers incomes. More people are not working, earning less income, and paying fewer taxes. However, politicians rarely cut government spending or contract government programs. Furthermore, laws prevent state and local governments from operating budget deficits. Thus, politicians must raise taxes to maintain government spending, creating financial instability. State and local governments always experience a financial crisis during economic downturns. Then they raise taxes on a faltering economy, which slows the economy even more.

For instance, the State of New York experienced a rapid increase in government spending as tax revenues poured in from Wall Street before the 2008 Financial Crisis. However, the crisis, which significantly slowed the financial markets and led to the bankruptcy of several large financial firms, including the loss of thousands of jobs on Wall Street, had a profound impact. With New York State supposedly receiving 25% of its tax revenue from Wall Street, the state was left with a staggering $14 billion budget deficit for 2009-2010, prompting the state to consider taxing a wide range of goods and services.

The U.S. real estate market experienced a boom between 2001 and 2007, with soaring property values leading to increased property tax collections by local governments. Flush with tax money, local government officials significantly expanded the size of local governments, undertaking projects such as building new jails and schools and hiring more police and teachers. However, the collapse of the housing bubble in 2007 had a devastating effect, particularly on Arizona, California, Florida, and Nevada, which saw the largest increases in property values and subsequently experienced the worst financial problems in the nation.

State governments imposed individual and corporate income taxes in two waves. The first wave occurred during the Great Depression. Twenty-six states passed a combination of personal and corporate taxes during the 1930s as our nation suffered during the Great Depression. The second wave happened during the 1960s and 1970s when seventeen states imposed income and corporate taxes. In the early 1970s, the Organization of Petroleum Exporting Countries (OPEC) withheld petroleum from the United States, causing petroleum prices to spike. Unfortunately, industries use petroleum in almost all products, such as gasoline, diesel, jet fuel, plastics, fertilizers, etc. Consequently, greater petroleum prices raised all prices in the economy, creating a supply shock and a recession. During a recession, tax revenue falls, which hurts the state governments. However, states always survive as they adopt income and corporate taxes to cover falling tax revenues.

Do we need more examples? Many states legalized lotteries to boost tax revenues. Politicians claim the lottery would fix public funding for education. Funding always helps until the next downturn in the economy. Then a state government invents new tax sources to compensate for budget shortfalls. The government is too stingy to make cuts or impose financial restraints on itself.

State governments also have financial instability on their expenditure side. Federal and state governments finance various social programs to help the elderly, poor, disabled, unemployed, and students. Instability source arises from the two states of the economy:

> ➤ **A Growing Economy:** Jobs become plentiful and easy to find. Consequently, people collect less unemployment, food stamps, welfare, and state health insurance, which reduces government expenditures. Unfortunately, politicians never save this money. They may reduce eligibility for state aid or expand social programs as states collect more significant tax revenues.

> ➤ **A Recession:** Jobs become scarce and difficult to find. Therefore, states spend more on social programs as people collect more unemployment, food stamps, welfare, and other public aid. A recession can bust budgets, and politicians usually tighten the requirements for these programs. Thus, states hike taxes to reduce their budget deficits. Increasing taxes during a recession weakens the recovery.

Property Taxes versus Income Taxes

Many people and organizations argue for eliminating state income taxes. They say that seven states do not have an income tax: Alaska, Florida, Nevada, South Dakota, Texas, Washington, and Wyoming. They believe a state eliminating its income tax would grow faster and create more jobs. We can check this premise by examining the state's economic data shown in Table 2.

The first statistic is the Tax Burden, which is the percentage of income that goes to the state and local government. Federal income taxes were excluded because high-income states, like Massachusetts, pay more federal income taxes than other states. The average tax burden for state and local governments 2009 was 9.8%. Seven states without state income taxes have a lower tax burden.

The State's Real Gross Domestic Product (GDP) is the second statistic. State GDP represents the total amount of goods and services produced in a state for a year. Real means analysts removed inflation's effect. Furthermore, growth in GDP means the state's economy expands, and the GDP is adjusted for a state's population, defined as GDP per capita. The average state GDP in 2009 was $41,808 per capita. All states have a higher GDP per capita than the average except Florida and Nevada. These two states were hit hard by a tsunami of foreclosures and high unemployment.

Table 2: 2008 State's Economic Characteristics

State	Tax Burden (%)	State Real GDP ($ per capita)	State Real GDP Growth Rate (%)	Unemployment Rate (%)
Alaska	6.3	62,243	8.9	7.7
Florida	9.2	35,321	-3.7	10.4
Nevada	7.5	41,418	-6.7	11.6
South Dakota	7.6	43,596	0.6	5.2
Texas	7.9	42,807	0.5	7.5
Washington	9.3	44,896	-2.4	10.2
Wyoming	7.8	61,214	9.8	6.3
Average	**9.8**	**41,808**	**-2.5**	**9.3**

Sources: Bureau of Economic Analysis, U.S. Department of Commerce; Bureau of Labor Statistics, U.S. Department of Labor; and The Tax Foundation.

The third statistic is the state's real GDP Growth Rate, which measures the percentage increase in the state's economy. The average state real GDP growth rate was 2.5% in 2009. All the states in Table 2 have a higher GDP growth rate than the average, except Florida and Nevada.

The last statistic is the Unemployment Rate, which the government defines as the percentage of workers who are unemployed and actively searching for work. The average unemployment rate was 9.3% in 2009. Florida, Nevada, and Washington have higher unemployment rates than the average. One must be careful because people migrate to more business-friendly states, which are the states with no state income taxes. Moreover, if a jobless person gives up his job search, then the government no longer considers this person unemployed and excludes this person from the unemployment statistics.

Data suggests five out of seven states with no income taxes are doing better than the national average. However, 2009 was just one year after the Great Recession. If we examine previous years, then this relationship weakens because a recession challenges the strength of a state's institutions.

Three factors weaken the relationship between no-income state taxes and economic growth:

> **Factor 1:** The average U.S. government tax burden was 26.6% in 2009, far exceeding the state's tax burden.

> **Factor 2:** Texas imposes a franchise tax on its businesses within the state, while Florida imposes a corporate tax. A corporate tax is a tax on a corporation's income, while a franchise tax is a tax on any business's income.

> **Factor 3:** States with income taxes rely on fines, fees, and property taxes, which are regressive taxes. Thus, regressive taxes hurt people with low incomes and older people more.

Property taxes are regressive. For example, the State of New Jersey is one of the most heavily taxed states in the nation, with the highest property taxes. Property taxes average nearly $8,000 annually on a house [9]. Someone on a fixed income must pay at least $666 monthly for property taxes. That is insane!

A property tax is an inherently unfair tax. Property taxes are based on housing market values, and selling one or two homes in the neighborhood establishes the market value for everyone else. Then the tax authority uses formulas to apply this market value to other homes in the neighborhood. The problem is that houses are unique and vary in condition. Some homes are new, while others are deteriorating and falling apart.

Property taxes are detrimental to industrial properties. Local government taxes the land, buildings, machines, and equipment. Then a bureaucrat determines the market value of large industrial machines. How do we place a market value on a 20-year-old, 10-ton press? Furthermore, property taxes are tied to a property's value, not a company's profits. Companies earning a loss still pay property taxes. At least with an income tax, a company earning a loss would pay lower taxes. Thus, property taxes put an industrial complex at a severe disadvantage.

The 2007 Great Recession will have an interesting impact on property taxes. As of 2012, housing market values continue falling. Thus, property taxes should also be falling, meaning local governments should lose tax revenue.

Local governments can do one or more of the following to prevent property taxes becoming lower:

> **First,** homeowners go through a process to dispute the value of their homes with the tax authorities. Local government can make the process difficult. Unfortunately, a court is at the end of the appeal process. The county government relies on property taxes to fund county courts. Thus, county courts have a financial incentive to maintain high property appraisals.

> **Second,** local governments could raise property tax rates. For local governments at their maximum constitutional tax rates, they could invent new taxes and fees.

> **Third,** if homes are not sold in a neighborhood, a homeowner cannot prove their house is losing value. Homeowners must prove their home's value becomes lower than the government's assessed value to get the government to reduce property taxes.

> **Fourth,** several local governments ignore the selling price of a foreclosed house. With foreclosed homes being discounted by 30% or more, local governments claim these sales represent exceptional cases.

Several states, like California, Idaho, Massachusetts, and Washington, use the home's last selling price to determine its value. This could be a good system, especially for the elderly who bought their homes 30 years ago. However, homeowners who purchased a home at the peak of the housing bubble are locked into high property values. Homebuyers can only escape these high property taxes by purchasing a new house for a lower price [4].

A government experiences greater financial exposure during economic downturns if it relies on numerous tax sources. For example, one state government has several small taxes while another imposes many taxes. When the economy enters a recession, the lower economic activity harms the state government more with the numerous taxes because that government experiences more declines across all revenue sources. This helps explain why states with no income taxes remain in better financial shape.

Conclusion

Capitalistic societies go through a life cycle. If a country has a capitalistic system with substantial private property rights and minimal interference from the government, it becomes more prosperous over time. A robust and rich society expands the tax base while the government becomes flush with more cash. As the government spends the tax revenue, the government establishes new bureaucracies and expands old ones. Consequently, a strong economy and expanding government create many good-paying jobs. However, the government has been developing regulations and increasing taxes over time. Eventually, too many rules and taxes become detrimental to the economy, causing incomes and business activity to fall. The problem is the government does not reduce its size, even if the population is falling or people are fleeing. Then the government enters a cycle of increasing taxes to make up for lower tax collections, causing society to stagnate and crumble.

The life cycle occurred in two southern states: Louisiana and Oklahoma. During the early 1980s, the Organization of Petroleum Exporting Countries raised the petroleum price vastly. As non-petroleum-producing states entered a recession, the petroleum-producing states, Louisiana and Oklahoma, were thriving. The petroleum industry created jobs, and the state governments collected large tax revenue flows. Then the states expanded their education system, expanded state government, and built massive prison systems. When the oil price went bust in the late 1980s, these states did not reduce the size of their governments. Instead, they imposed various tax hikes to sustain their high-level government spending that remains in effect today.

Life cycle occurred in the U.S. economy on a large scale. U.S. economy transformed from an industrial society to a service-oriented one. Our politicians claim our tax systems are antiquated and obsolete, and they must update them because taxes are based on a manufacturing economy and not a service-oriented one. They argue that the government exempts many services from taxes.

Our politicians have a flaw in their reasoning. The U.S. manufacturing sector left the United States from high taxes and excessive regulations, while the service-oriented sector prospered under low taxes. A government subjects a manufacturing company to the following taxes:

> **Income Taxes:** A business pays federal, state, county, and city income taxes. These taxes vary by jurisdiction.

> **Corporate Taxes:** The United States imposes separate taxes on corporations. Tax rates vary from 15 to 35% [10], making the United States one of the highest taxes in the world. Corporations file various tax credits to reduce their tax burdens.

> **Social Security and Medicare Taxes:** Employees pay approximately 6% to Social Security and roughly 1% to Medicare. These are matching taxes because employers match the amount the employees pay.

> **Property Taxes:** The government levies property taxes on land, machines, equipment, and buildings. Consequently, the government taxes high-tech and capital-intensive industries heavily through property taxes.

> **Workers' Disability Compensation:** States determine the insurance rates, which makes them a tax because businesses must buy this insurance that states manage.

> **Unemployment Insurance:** States determine the rates. The state forces employers to pay this insurance and administers this program. This is a tax.

➢ **Mandated Benefits:** Businesses must provide medical insurance and pensions to full-time employees. Thus, many service-oriented businesses rely on part-time labor to avoid paying these benefits and reduce costs.

Moving to China can help manufacturing companies avoid these taxes and lower their tax burden. Furthermore, China has cheap labor and lax regulations. One of the largest corporations in the world, Wal-Mart, can compete with all retailers in terms of price with its cheap Chinese products.

References

[1] McHugh, Jack and Steve Stanek. November 1, 2004. "'Shift-and-Shaft' Tax Proposal Ekes out Win in Michigan." *Budget and Tax News.* Available at www.heartland.org (access date: 01/04/2010).
[2] Gordon, Marcy. November 13, 2009. "Banks will have to prepay insurance fees." *The South Bend Tribune.*
[3] Chamberlain, Andrew. June 12, 2006. "Is California's Tax Base Preparing to Flee?" *Tax Foundation.*
[4] Christie, Les. October 14, 2008. "Home prices may plummet, but taxes won't." *CNN.* Available at www.cnnmoney.com (access date: 10/15/08).
[5] Mumford, Lou. February 13, 2004. "Michigan stores fear smokers will head south." *South Bend Tribune.*
[6] Becsi, Zsolt. 2000. "The Shifty Laffer Curve." *Economic Review – Federal Reserve Bank of Atlanta* 85(3): 53- 64.
[7] Laffer, Arthur B. June 1, 2004. "The Laffer Curve: Past, Present, and Future." *The Heritage Foundation.* Available at www.heritage.org (access date: 3/23/07).
[8] Federal Highway Administration. September 1999. Federal Tax Rates on Motor Fuels and Lubricating Oils. Washington, DC: U.S. Department of Transportation, Table FE-101A. Available at http://www.fhwa.dot.gov/ohim/hs98/tables/fe101a.pdf (access date: 8/14/06).
[9] Summers, Pat. June 5, 2008. "Homeowners Demand Tax Reassessments As Market Values Plummet." *eFinanceDirectory.*
[10] Internal Revenue Code. 26 United States Code 11. Available at http://www.law.cornell.edu/uscode/html/uscode26/usc_sec_26_00000011----000-.html (access date: 1/30/2012).

6. Corrupt Police and Kangaroo Courts

"When men are pure, laws are useless; when men are corrupt, laws are broken."

-Benjamin Disraeli

The traditional role of the police is to protect and serve the public. However, local and state governments changed the role of their police force. The government encourages police to write and issue more citations and tickets, pursuing revenue. Political leaders assure us that police do not have quotas and that issuing tickets is a money loser for the government [1]. Nevertheless, why do police write citations or arrest people for silly infractions of the law? Several examples include:

- ➤ **Example 1:** In Washington, D.C., the police arrested a woman for eating a candy bar in the subway [2].

- ➤ **Example 2:** Police in Georgia cited a woman for operating a vehicle without a driver's license. A woman with cerebral palsy drives her electric wheelchair to work on the shoulder of a road. Police also threatened to impound her wheelchair [3].

- ➤ **Example 3:** In New York City, police issued a citation for a pregnant woman sitting on the subway steps [1].

- ➤ **Example 4:** In Galveston, Texas, code enforcement cited restaurant owners for displaying the hours of operation because this violated historic preservation ordinances.

- ➤ **Example 5:** On December 3, 2005, Charles Atherton was walking across a street and was hit by a car in Washington, D.C. The strong impact knocked him out of his shoes, and his head hit the windshield. As he lay there waiting for the ambulance, a policeman wrote Charles a $5 jaywalking ticket. Police claimed he was conscious and was outside the crosswalk [4].

These examples illustrate the police are more aggressive, and they write tickets for minor offenses. City, state, and the federal government keep hiring more police officers and agents. If criminals are not committing crimes, police cannot sit around and wait. They must arrest people and write tickets. Thus, each person sitting in a jail cell or each ticket sent to a court proves the police officers are working.

The criminal justice system does not care whether the violations are minor. Moreover, the criminal justice system can easily classify minor crimes as serious ones. For example, police and prosecutors have charged people for assaulting a police officer because they growled at a police dog. Even an Ohio appeals court ruled that barking at a police dog is not illegal [5].

Why do local, state, and federal governments hire more agents and police officers? First, these government agencies keep passing laws, and someone must enforce those laws. Government officials want complete compliance with their regulations, although they are likely to violate their laws. Thus, the more rules a society has, the more citizens will break these rules [6], necessitating a state to hire a large group of police and enforcers. Second, the media scares the public by focusing on crime daily. The public believes crime is soaring even though violent crime has been decreasing since the 1990s.

Several examples show the state expanding the size and scope of laws:

> **Example 1:** Police arrested an 80-year-old woman for feeding ducks in Lynn, Massachusetts. An elderly woman violated a city ordinance, although she has fed the ducks for 45 years [7].

> **Example 2:** States established food police, who threaten, harass, and arrest people who grow and sell organic foods or donate food to the homeless. In 2012, staff at a school in North Carolina confiscated a girl's lunch that she had

brought from home. The school forced the girl to eat processed food from the cafeteria [8].

> **Example 3:** The City of Canton, Ohio, passed a new law where the city can incarcerate its citizens for not mowing their lawns. A second violation of tall grass becomes a misdemeanor [9]. How will the city enforce this law? Will police officers drive around and measure the height of everyone's grass? Of course, the enforcement officers will avoid the poor neighborhoods but will heavily patrol the middle-class neighborhoods. The middle class will likely pay the fines, while the rich may have strong connections to the political leaders and will complain about police harassment.

> **Example 4:** In 2000, the State of Oklahoma expanded the definition of drinking under the influence (DUI). For instance, if an intoxicated person walks home with his car keys in his pocket, then the state can charge him with a DUI. Possession of car keys implies a person intended to drive drunk. If a person does drink too much, then the best thing for society is for that person to walk home and not drive, but Oklahoma is one of those states that love incarcerating its citizens.

Contrary to what government officials say, the government does not lose money for writing tickets or arresting people. First, the government collects taxes for police officers, prosecutors, judges, jails, and prisons. Taxpayers pay these expenses. Second, any money collected for fines or fees is extra for the government. City and state governments vary where this money goes. Money could be deposited into the general fund or for new police equipment. Of course, some states like Louisiana, Oklahoma, and Texas built massive prison systems, which require enormous amounts of funding.

In one extreme case, the police in Tenaha, Texas, are highway pirates. Police pull over unsuspecting motorists and charge them with a crime. Prosecutors agreed to drop the criminal charges if the motorists agreed and waived their right to their property. Police seize cars, jewelry, cash, cell phones, and sneakers. Mayor George Bowers defended the actions of the police by stating, "It's always helpful to have any kind of income to expand our police force." The mayor wants additional money to add a second police car and expand the police department [10]. Then we know what comes next. More police means they can pull over more motorists and steal more property.

The crowning achievement of our criminal justice system was the arrest of George Norris, who was arrested for importing and selling banned orchids. However, he did not break the law because his orchids were not on the banned list. Nevertheless, the federal government spent months investigating George and dispatched a team of armed agents to search his home and business. Instead of apologizing to him, the federal government sent him to a federal prison for mistakes in his paperwork. Judge stated, "Life sometimes presents us with lemons… turn lemons into lemonade" [11].

The Orchid case caused a small public outcry about the overcriminalization of our laws. Our government subjects us to many laws that are open to broad interpretation. Consequently, many Americans could be imprisoned for breaking any of these laws.

The Race to Incarcerate

A problem evolves when a country's laws, rules, and regulations become too numerous and complicated. Consequently, the government finds more people violating the law. Of course, the United States uses incarceration to punish people, and incarceration rates have skyrocketed by 500% since the 1970s. Several states adopted themes like "get tough on crime", "the war on drugs," and "three strikes, and you're out," causing incarceration rates to surge [12]. These catchy phrases and slogans suggest states are in a race to incarcerate.

Figure 1 shows the incarceration and violent crime rates, where the federal and state governments are incarcerating more people while violent crime is decreasing. The incarceration rate is the number of prisoners serving time in federal and state prisons and county jails. The violent crime index is the total number of murders, manslaughter, forcible rapes, robberies, and aggravated assaults. Both rates are adjusted for population changes and expressed per 100,000 persons. Furthermore, the incarceration rate does not include defendants sitting in jail, waiting for their trial.

Figure 1: U.S. Incarceration Rate versus the Crime Rate

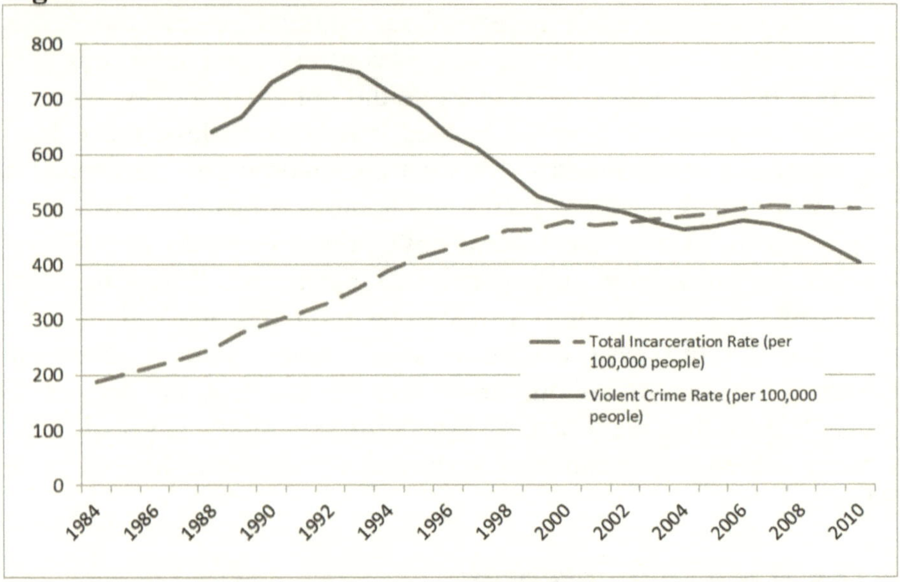

Sources: Bureau of Justice Statistic and Federal Bureau of Investigation

The government incarcerates people to improve society by removing individuals who severely violate society's rules. Initially, a prison was a place for criminals to think about their crimes and ask God for forgiveness. Penitent is the root word for penitentiary. However, prisons evolved into warehouses that store malcontents and felons. Several states sponsor psychological treatment for inmates and offer a chance to complete a college degree. Nevertheless, these programs do not work because the recidivism rate hovers around 67%. Thus, on average, seven inmates out of 10 will return to prison [13].

Why do the federal and state governments lock people up? It is not a vast conspiracy! Police, judges, and prosecutors locate, convict, and incarcerate people. That is their job! Like everyone else, they want job security and higher wages. If the police arrest fewer people, prosecutors file fewer dockets, and judges hear fewer cases, they cannot run to the legislature and request more funding. If the amount of work the criminal justice system does is declining, their funding should decrease. For the criminal justice system to continue expanding, they must arrest, prosecute, and incarcerate more people so they can beg more money from the legislature. Thus, Parkinson's Law applies to the criminal justice system, too.

Society pays a significant cost if it incarcerates numerous people. The total costs include the following:

> **Cost 1:** States must pay for the incarceration with tax revenue. They spend an average of $23,876 per year to lock one person up in 2005 [14].

> **Cost 2:** The criminal justice system removes a potential taxpayer from society. This person does not earn wages or pay taxes. The key word is potential because some criminals are deadbeats who do not work.

> **Cost 3:** The government diverts public funds from other programs like education and social programs. Thus, prisons and the criminal justice system compete against other government agencies for tax dollars, such as schools, parks, universities, and food stamps.

Table 1 shows the 2009 incarceration rates for the states with the five highest and five lowest incarceration rates. The average incarceration rate in 2009 for the United States was 442 per 100,000 persons, which excludes the federal government. Unfortunately, the states with the highest incarceration rates have a low portion of their population with a high school diploma or higher, except Oklahoma. Furthermore, the highest incarceration states have the lowest school funding per pupil, except Louisiana. The pattern reverses for states with the lowest incarceration rates. These states have a higher portion of citizens with a high school diploma and higher, except Rhode Island, and have more considerable funding per pupil, except North Dakota.

Table 1: 2009 Incarceration Rates versus Public School Funding

State	Incarceration Rate (per 100,000)	High School Graduates or more (% population)	School Funding ($ per pupil)
Highest Incarceration Rates			
Alabama	650	82.1	9,321
Louisiana	881	82.2	11,413
Mississippi	702	80.4	7,814
Oklahoma	657	85.6	8,249
Texas	648	79.9	9,143
Lowest Incarceration Rates			
Maine	150	90.2	14,576
Minnesota	189	91.5	11,663
New Hampshire	206	91.3	13,130
North Dakota	228	90.1	10,805
Rhode Island	211	84.7	16,127
Average	**442**	**85.3**	**10,905**

Sources: Bureau of Justice Statistics and 2010 Statistical Abstract of the United States

Table 2 shows a weaker pattern for higher education. States with higher incarceration rates have fewer college graduates as a percentage of their population, while the states with the lowest incarceration rates have a higher percentage of educated citizens. However, state college funding is a paradox. States with the highest incarceration rates grant larger funding to higher education that exceeds the state average, except Alabama. Meanwhile, the lowest incarceration states grant lower college funding than the average, except North Dakota. An answer to this paradox is states with the highest incarceration rates have fewer full-time college students so that they can fund higher education at a greater level.

Table 2: 2009 Incarceration Rates versus College Funding

State	Incarceration Rate (per 100,000)	Four Years of College or More (% of population)	College Funding ($ per full-time student)
Highest Incarceration Rates			
Alabama	650	22.0	5,574
Louisiana	881	21.4	6,567
Mississippi	702	19.6	6,473
Oklahoma	657	22.7	6,914
Texas	648	25.5	7,622
Lowest Incarceration Rates			
Maine	150	26.9	6,331
Minnesota	189	31.5	5,957
New Hampshire	206	32.0	3,229
North Dakota	228	25.8	6,525
Rhode Island	211	30.5	5,250
Average	**442**	**27.9**	**6,454**

Sources: Bureau of Justice Statistics and 2010 Statistical Abstract of the United States

State governments have built too many prisons, compounding the incarceration rate. When a state builds a brand-new prison, state officials have an obligation to fill it. Otherwise, the taxpayers become furious because the state wasted funding on a new empty prison. The criminal justice system may incarcerate innocent people or elevate minor crimes into major ones, requiring prison sentences to fill these prisons. This problem is repeated in many county governments because counties continually build new jails and facilities that quickly become overcrowded.

Why do states build so many prisons? It cannot be the violent crime rate falling since the early 1990s. State governments build more prisons because politicians do not want to appear soft on crime. Furthermore, states wish for economic development. Opening a new jail in a small, stagnant community could cause an inflow of federal and state dollars, thus providing jobs and economic growth.

Prisons, however, contribute little to local economic growth or create few jobs in a community. Prison supplies are specialized, and local suppliers do not supply them. Moreover, prisons hire a limited number of guards, and local governments may divert funding from other public investments because they must invest in roads and utilities for the prison [15]. Therefore, prisons may be a terrible source of economic development for a small community.

Administrating Justice

The police are the first contact with the criminal justice system. They investigate crimes, arrest perpetrators, and provide critical information to the judges and prosecutors. Thus, a natural question arises. If police are protecting the public, why do police sometimes violently attack innocent citizens? The following includes examples of police brutality:

> **Example 1:** Three policemen beat up a retired black school teacher in New Orleans, Louisiana, in October 2005. The police even threw one bystander onto a car because he was filming the incident. The retired schoolteacher was charged with public intoxication, battery on a police officer, and resisting arrest [16]. The videotape clearly shows the schoolteacher on the ground as four police officers violently kicked and struck him.

> **Example 2:** In a small Louisiana town, a white cop tasered a 240-pound black man nine times, although the defendant was handcuffed. The officer claimed the man did not move fast enough. The police chief replied the officer could either set him free, taser him, or shoot him. Tasing was the best option because officers do not let criminals go [17]. Is the police chief stupid? Tasers shoot out probes that stick to a person's body and jolt suspects between 20,000 and 150,000 volts of electricity [18]. How fast could we move if the police tasered us multiple times?

> ➢ **Example 3:** Brothers were filming sheriff deputies in 2002 as they raided a neighbor's house in Houston, Texas. The deputies did not like being filmed, so they charged into that family's house with guns drawn, threatening to shoot the brothers. Then they took the videotape. The deputies arrested the brothers who filmed them and charged them with resisting arrest. Police even destroyed the tapes. Luckily, the falsely arrested brothers settled a lawsuit from Harris County for $1.7 million [19]. Harris County Sheriff's Department became so angry over this lawsuit that they placed the brothers under police surveillance. The public became enraged, and the Sheriff's Department had to disband their surveillance unit [20, 21].

Does it matter that citizens are photographing or videotaping the police? If the police do their duty and do the right thing, a videotape only enhances their actions. Unfortunately, police abuse will become worse because courts and the government are removing the checks on police power.

Legislatures pass more laws, transferring more power to prosecutors and police. With this transfer of power, police can quickly arrest a person for minor violations or bring up false charges. Every time a police officer attacked a citizen, the prosecutor charged the citizen with resisting arrest.

Politicians and bureaucrats assure us that they are protecting the public, but the government uses national security and public safety as arguments to take over its society, creating a police state. Remember the adage—power corrupts, and absolute power corrupts absolutely. As the criminal justice system gains more power, we will see more and more abuse by our judicial system and police.

The government and courts continually expand police powers over time. For example, forty years ago, all states had no seat belt laws. Drivers and occupants could decide whether to wear seat belts. Then legislators and governors passed seat belt laws because wearing seatbelts increases the chances of a person surviving a car accident.

On the surface, the government portrays it cares for its people by protecting them. However, seat belt laws embed a hidden agenda: The police can issue citations for not wearing seatbelts, providing another revenue stream for the government. (Of course, the court system wants us to pay the seat belt fine rather than be concerned for our well-being.)

One person in a car who does not wear a seatbelt gives the police the power to pull that car over and investigate it. Police can determine whether the occupants have violated other laws. In the old days, we educated people about the benefits of using seatbelts and then gave them free choice, whether they wanted to use them or not. Consequently, courts rarely keep police powers in check.

Several reasons include the following:

➢ **Reason 1:** Courts evolved into bloated bureaucracies that need and consume financial resources. Police need time to write reports; a prosecutor needs time to review the report, and a judge needs time to review a case. All this time is expensive! If a judge acquits a defendant, the judge has no basis to collect fines. Furthermore, the criminal justice system does not look good if it has a large percentage of cases where the judges acquitted the defendants. How could the criminal justice system request the legislature for additional money if they are arresting innocent people?

➢ **Reason 2:** The press and news give the public a false impression that crime is rampant and rising. Judges must find the defendants guilty so they do not appear weak and soft on crime.

➢ **Reason 3:** Courts operate like a factory. Every day, the sheriff's deputies round up defendants and line them in front of the judge, like cattle at the slaughterhouse. With the dockets complete, courts can encourage, coerce, and frighten defendants to plead guilty and send them to numerous agencies, like probation offices, counseling programs, and forced volunteer work for non-profit agencies.

> **Reason 4:** In small communities, the municipal court, prosecutor's office, and police are housed in the same building. They see each other daily and may be friends outside of the city government. Defendants are outsiders that judges must find guilty of their crimes.

Municipal and county courts usually rule in favor of the enforcement agencies. It makes no difference if the police lied, withheld evidence, or violated a defendant's rights. Courts excuse an officer's behavior. If the police are never punished for lying, withholding evidence, or violating the defendant's rights, then nothing keeps an abusive police force in check. Numerous cases bring this fact to life:

> **Case 1:** Problems plagued the City of Houston's Police Crime Lab. The Federal government closed the DNA section of the lab in 2003 because 93 cases had "serious issues." Investigators also found problems with the analysis of firearms, narcotics, and body fluids. Investigators placed the blame on incompetent lab technicians and the need to tailor reports to find defendants guilty [22].

A defendant could spend thousands of dollars to re-test the evidence. Thus, shoddy, fraudulent lab work would rarely be exposed in most court cases. This is not an isolated problem. Problems were found with the City of Oklahoma City Crime Lab, FBI Crime Labs, and state crime labs for California, Florida, Illinois, Montana, and Washington [23].

> **Case 2:** In Tulia, Texas, one law enforcement officer wanted an excellent arrest record and was also a racist, thief, and liar. He arrested 43 minorities, claiming the minorities sold him cocaine. The officer provided no evidence other than his word. Minorities received harsh sentences, and the officer received the Texas Department of Public Safety's 1999 Outstanding Lawman of the Year.

Cracks appeared in the officer's story because judges dropped charges against five defendants. When the drug sales occurred, two defendants were at work. One was in another state at a bank, and the other had inaccurate descriptions. Eventually, Rick Perry, the Texas Governor, pardoned the 35 minorities, and the defendants settled for a meager lump sum of $250,000, agreeing not to sue the county government [24, 25].

> **Case 3:** In Berwyn Heights, Maryland, the mayor returned home and saw a package on his porch. He carried the package into his home, and seconds later, the SWAT team crashed through the mayor's front door and shot his two dogs. Unfortunately, someone mailed a box containing 32 pounds of marijuana to the mayor's house [26].

> **Case 4:** In Dallas, Texas, a drug informant planted cocaine into people's vehicles. However, he crushed sheetrock, making it look like cocaine. Fifty-nine people of Mexican descent were charged with drug charges. Several defendants took plea deals, and others were deported until two defense attorneys uncovered the truth and tested the substances for cocaine [27].

> **Case 5:** The last case is undercover detectives chopped-up macadamia nuts. Then the detectives sold the chopped nuts to drug users because they looked identical to crack cocaine. Consequently, judges imposed harsh, long prison sentences for cocaine offenses. Unfortunately, the keyword for convictions is intent and not reality. Although people can possess macadamia nuts legally, the buyers thought they had purchased cocaine [28]. Thus, the taxpayers paid the bill to lock up these criminals for buying nuts.

These cases are not isolated, independent examples. The criminal justice system has convicted innocent people for crimes across the United States. Some of the cases above came from police task forces. A task force involves several police agencies that are formed to tackle a particular crime, such as drug trafficking and prostitution rings.

The problem is that a task force receives funding from the United States government and from property seizures. Thus, a task force must show results. That is why forming these task forces is dangerous! If a task force forms to find drug traffickers, then agents must find drug traffickers. Otherwise, a failed mission jeopardizes federal funding and a failure of the government agency [27]. Sometimes, police officers fabricate evidence and convict innocent people rather than admit a public failure.

Innocent defendants can appeal their fraudulent convictions to a higher court because every defendant has the right to an appeal. However, the government does not tell us it takes time and money. Appealing a wrongful conviction could cost a few thousand dollars and take several years. Tulia, Texas, only appeared in the spotlight because *The Texas Observer* and *Time* magazine wrote articles about Tulia, causing intense scrutiny.

States create another problem by releasing criminal records. A fraudulent conviction appears on a person's criminal record. It shows a person's charge, court outcome, and any appeals. A criminal record never states that the police fabricated evidence or that a judge railroaded a person to prison. Wrongful convictions can trail a person for the rest of his life.

Judges do not hesitate to throw innocent people into jail, but they will play favorites and exonerate fellow members of the criminal justice system. For example, a Cleburne, Texas, judge threw out the blood-alcohol test results for State District Judge Elizabeth Berry. The judge ruled that police did not have sufficient evidence to search this judge, although she drove 27 MPH above the speed limit, had numerous empty beer cans in her car, and had her breath wreaked of alcohol. Consequently, the charges were dropped because of insufficient evidence [29]. Regular citizens would rightly spend time in jail if they did this.

The State Protection of Children

All states have passed laws to protect the children because some parents abuse their children. Thus, the state should intervene and remove the children. However, many decent, loving families have lost custody of their children because caseworkers cannot distinguish between actual child abuse and alleged cases of child abuse. Any vindictive, bitter relative or acquaintance can falsely report child abuse to a hotline, and a caseworker must investigate this allegation. Furthermore, the state never releases the callers' identities. State child abuse hotlines received 3.3 million reports in 2005, and most reports were found not to be true. Parents were reported to the state for spanking children, homeschooling, or accidental injury [30].

Four factors cause child-protective services to be aggressive with parents. The factors include the following:

> **Factor 1:** Parkinson's Law also applies to child-protective agencies because they employ many professionals, like caseworkers, lawyers, and therapists [30]. For these professionals to request more funding, they must process more cases. Hence, they must find more and more children in need of services.

> **Factor 2:** States leverage funding from the federal government. In every case the state processes, the federal government reimburses the states for some of their costs. Thus, a state tries to maximize the number of child abuse cases and, therefore, the cash flow from the federal government [30].

> **Factor 3:** The state enters the names of suspected parents into a state database for child abuse. If parents are entered into this database multiple times, then the state could automatically take custody of the kids, even if the state has no proof of child abuse.

> **Factor 4:** Child-protective services and courts have poor oversight [30]. Since child abuse involves children, judges throw many of the standard criminal rights out the window. Parents cannot request jury trials or question children on the stand. Furthermore, the judges seal the court records, hiding their decisions from public scrutiny. In extreme cases, caseworkers can coax or trick children into saying anything on a video camera. Then caseworkers present the videotape as evidence, which the defense cannot cross-examine.

The current system is not necessarily flawed as long as the judges, caseworkers, and therapists are honest and genuinely want to help families. Then judges are not likely to take custody of children for false allegations. However, greed and Parkinson's Laws still apply. The following cases illustrate this point:

> **Case 1:** Two judges in Philadelphia received payoffs from a private youth detention center. The judges received $2.6 million and sentenced juveniles for minor offenses to long terms in this youth treatment facility [31]. Youth detention centers charge the government at least $100 per day.

> **Case 2:** Many blogs on the internet complain about abuse from child-protective services. For example, child welfare investigators in one county, Contra Costa County, California, supposedly terrorized families. Once a family appeared on the radar, investigators would continually harass them.

The government will punish a government agency if the public protests loud enough. For instance, Contra Costa County experienced a financial crisis in 2008, and many families appeared at the county hearings and complained loudly about Child-Protective Services. Consequently, the county commissioners decimated this department, laying off 75 caseworkers. However, the county decimated other departments, too, in 2008.

Conclusion

Public officials are so worked up over crime and the need to pass laws and hire police officers that some local governments destroyed their budgets. For example, Vallejo, California, has a population of 120,000 and is located near San Francisco. The city filed for Chapter 9 bankruptcy because city officials could not control their spending. The city has an operating fund of $87 million, with police and fire departments comprising 75% of the city budget [32]. Consequently, politicians and bureaucrats will hire more police officers and build more prisons and jails until it busts their budget.

The government fails to understand that incarcerating people for minor offenses can destroy people economically. If a judge incarcerates a person in jail for a month because he cannot pay his fine, like wearing the wrong clothes for jogging – a crime in Stillwater, Oklahoma – then that person could lose his job. After a job loss, that person loses his car and home while homelessness waits around the corner. That person also has a criminal record, severely hindering him from finding new employment. Furthermore, the government still wants to collect the court fees, fines, and cost of incarceration, although it destroys a person's life.

An ever-expanding police state fuels hatred between the government and its people. Unfortunately, the government does not understand that it cannot lock up everybody, which is why police states have short lives.

Many states started the dangerous trend to force inmates to pay for their incarceration. An overzealous and cash-hungry judicial system will incarcerate more people for silly infractions of the law. Charging inmates for incarceration produces the following three outcomes:

> ➤ **Outcome 1:** Police officers have an incentive to jail more people. Although violent crime rates have fallen since the 1990s, the judicial system packs jails and prisons for minor infractions.

> **Outcome 2:** The court system has a strong financial incentive to find the defendant guilty. If the court does not find the person guilty, it cannot charge the defendant's room and board for jail.

> **Outcome 3:** Society enters a vicious cycle if the government fills its jails and prisons with inmates to capacity. The government keeps building new jails and filling them with more violators. Then with a falling crime rate, the government must expand the laws to produce more criminals.

The 2008 Financial Crisis brings another complication. The U.S. economy is losing jobs. Unemployment and poverty are climbing while people lose hope. Some inmates refuse to be released from jail, while others deliberately commit crimes, so the state locks them up. The state pays for room, food, and, in some cases, medical care. This is a problem in Detroit, Michigan [33], which will quickly spread to other cities as the U.S. economy continues stagnating.

References

[1] Archibold, Randal C. and Nichole M. Christian. June 4, 2003. "To Embattled Mayor, Tickets Are the Hottest Issue in Town." *The New York Times*.

[2] Associated Press. July 29, 2004. "Candy bar lands woman in police custody." *Houston Chronicle*.

[3] theNewspaper.com. March 14, 2008. "Georgia: Traffic Cop Tickets Wheelchair." Available at www.theNewspaper.com (access date: 9/25/08).

[4] Associated Press. December 3, 2005. "Man hit by car gets jaywalking ticket." *Houston Chronicle*.

[5] Loewe, Wayne. April 4, 2003. "Barking at police dogs is not illegal." *Court TV*.

[6] Morgan, Theodore. 1964. "The Theory of Error in Centrally-Directed Economic Systems." *The Quarterly Journal of Economics* 78(3): 395-419.

[7] *Treehugger*. December 10, 2011. "80-Year-Old Woman Jailed for Feeding Ducks After Doing It for 45 Years." Available at http://www.treehugger.com/culture/meet-80-year-old-woman-who-criminal-duck-feeder-video.html (access date 4/23/12).

[8] Huff, Ethan A. March 2, 2012. "Parents protest freedom-crushing food police who search lunch bags of schoolchildren." Available at

http://www.naturalnews.com/035123_food_police_lunch_bags_schoolchild
ren.html (access date 4/23/2012).

[9] Associated Press. June 3, 2008. "Ohio city OKs jail time for failing to mow lawn." *Houston Chronicle*.

[10] Sandberg, Lisa. February 7, 2009. "Property seizure by police called 'highway piracy'" *Houston Chronicle*.

[11] *The Washington Times*. October 5, 2000. "Criminalizing everyone." Available at http://www.washingtontimes.com/news/2009/oct/05/criminalizing-everyone/?page=all (access date 4/24/12).

[12] Shelden, Randall G. 2004. "The Imprisonment Crisis in America: Introduction." *Review of Policy Research* 21(1): 5-12.

[13] Bureau of Justice Statistics. 2002. "In a 15 State study, over two-thirds of released prisoners were rearrested within three years." Available at http://www.ojp.usdoj.gov/bjs/reentry/recidivism.htm (access date 01/09/09).

[14] Aizenman, N.C. February 29, 2008. "The high cost of incarceration." *The Washington Post*. Available at http://www.denverpost.com/ci_8400051 (access date 01/02/09).

[15] Hooks, Gregory, Clayton Mosher, Thomas Rotolo, and Linda Lobao. March 2004. "The Prison Industry: Carceral Expansion and Employment in U.S. Counties,1969–1994." *Social Science Quarterly* 85(1): 37-57.

[16] Simon, Dan, Alina Cho, Terry Frieden, Rod Griola, Chris Strathmann, Jeanne Meserve, and Susan Candiotti. October 12, 2005. "Beating victim: No anger toward police." *CNN*.

[17] Griffin, Drew and David Fitzpatrick. July 22, 2008. "Man dies after cop hits him with Taser 9 times." *CNN*. Available at www.CNN.com/Crime (access date 7/11/08).

[18] Harris, Tom. 2008. "How Stun Guns Work." *Howstuffworks*. Available at http://electronics.howstuffworks.com/stun-gun3.htm (access date: 12/24/08).

[19] Miller, Carlos. March 9, 2008. "Houston brothers receive $1.7 million in wrongful arrest suit." Photography is not a crime. Available from http://carlosmiller.com/

[20] O'hare, Peggy. June 3, 2008. "Under fire, Sheriff's Office disbands surveillance unit." *Houston Chronicle*.

[21] Texas Cable News. May 19, 2008. "Some lawmakers want Texas AG to investigate Harris County Sheriff's Office." *KHOU News*. Available from http://www.txcn.com/

[22] Khanna, Roma and Steve McVicker. May 12, 2006. "Police lab tailored tests to theories, report says." *Houston Chronicle*.

[23] Maier, Timothy W. June 2003. "Inside the DNA Labs." *Insight Mag*. Available at www.insightmag.com (access date: 7/11/08).

[24] Sherrer, Hans. "Travesty in Tulia, Texas: Frame-up of 38 Innocent People Orchestrated by a County Sheriff, Prosecutor and Judge." Available at www.forejustice.org (accessed on 7/3/08).

[25] *Drug Policy Alliance*. 2008. "Drugs, Policy, and the Law – Tulia, Texas." Available at http://www.drugpolicy.org/law/police/tulia/index.cfm (access date: 02/05/08)

[26] Zongker, Brett. August 8, 2008. "Police clear name of Md. mayor after drug raid." *Yahoo News*.

[27] *DRCNet Foundation*. February 2, 2002. "Backlash Emerges as Texas Drug Task Forces Run Amok." The Drug Reform Coordination Network (DRCNet). Available at StoptheDrugWar.org (access date 7/11/08).

[28] *Wikipedia.org*. "Crack Cocaine." Available at http://en.wikipedia.org/wiki/Crack_cocaine (access date 08/22/2010).

[29] Associated Press. January 23, 2009. "Texas Judge's Blood-Alcohol Test Inadmissible." *Houston Chronicle*.

[30] Hahn, Bill. July 11, 2007. "Family Attorney Blows the Whistle on State Child Protective Services Agencies." *The T.R.U.T.H. Project*.

[31] Hurdle, Jon. February 13, 2009. "U.S. judges admit to jailing children for money." *Reuters*.

[32] *The Canadian Press*. May 25, 2008. "California city that is in bankruptcy may become the model for others."

[33] Crary, David and Corey Williams. December 26, 2008. "Detroit replaces New Orleans as most beleaguered American city." *South Florida Times*. Available at http://www.sfltimes.com/index.php?option=com_content&task=view&id=2273&Itemid=42 (access date 01/02/09).

7. Eroding the Bill of Rights

"A man will fight harder for his interests than for his rights."
-Napoleon Bonaparte

Thirteen colonies had just won the Revolutionary War, which separated the colonies from the King of England. They were afraid to establish a new, strong centralized government. The states believed that if they created a strong centralized government, it would become powerful and eventually usurp power from the state governments. Consequently, Congress ratified the Bill of Rights to appease the states, limiting the power of the United States government.

The Bill of Rights is a powerful document because it limits the federal government's power. The Bill of Rights originally applied to the federal government, but through a Supreme Court case, Gitlow versus New York in 1925, was the Bill of Rights applied to the states. The Supreme Court upheld the conviction of Benjamin Gitlow, who was a socialist and advocated the overthrow of the government. The Supreme Court ruled that speech and writings supporting the overthrow of the government did not violate the free speech clause of the First Amendment.

The Bill of Rights is a piece of paper that cannot impose limits on the government. Only government officials can limit their power. The Bill of Rights helped restrain the government's power for 200 years because it imbued a set of ethics and duties on politicians, judges, Presidents, governors, and legislators. However, the government circumvented the Bill of Rights through the acts of Congress, Presidents, and the federal courts. Unfortunately, the states' nightmare has come true. The federal government has usurped control and power away from the states.

States are not big on the Bill of Rights either. They are becoming as oppressive as the U.S. federal government. For example, after the terrorist attacks on the World Trade Center on September 11, 2001, the state police and the FBI could brand a U.S. citizen as a terrorist if he quoted the Bill of Rights. If a citizen cannot quote the laws that the government officials and agents supposedly must follow, then the laws no longer exist.

We write each amendment of the Bill of Rights as a section heading and explain how the federal or state government has circumvented it.

Amendment I

"Congress shall make no law respecting an establishment of religion, or prohibiting the free exercise thereof; or abridging the freedom of speech, or of the press; or the right of the people peaceably to assemble, and to petition the Government for a redress of grievances" [1].

The judicial system has severely abused, twisted, and distorted this Amendment. This Amendment aims to protect religion and a free press. The Founding Fathers did not intend for the American people to be atheists nor remove God from public institutions. They did not want the federal government to sponsor a particular religion. With the United States being a melting pot of different cultures, the Founding Fathers wanted people to choose their religion, whether it was Catholic, Presbyterian, Lutheran, Baptist, or Judaism.

The Founding Fathers did not want a godless, atheistic society because religion has power. For example, if 99% of the U.S. population believed in God and the Ten Commandments, we would have a society with a tiny government. Religion is a source of discipline and behavior control.

The federal government has contributed to the deterioration of society. The U.S. government successfully eliminated religion from society. It encourages the breakup of traditional families and helps finance out-of-wedlock children. What have we achieved? The government builds more prisons, court buildings, jails, and treatment facilities. The U.S. incarceration rate is 2% of the U.S. population, and the federal and state governments are rapidly going broke. However, crime still occurs.

The courts have expanded freedom of the press to cover all kinds of behavior. We have the freedom to walk naked. Nudists want to walk around without clothes: Pornography is viewed as free speech. College professors have the freedom to grade students. In the 8th

U.S. Federal District Court, we can give a cop the middle finger. (Interpretation of laws can differ among federal court districts until a Supreme Court decision brings all districts to the same consensus).

Judges forgot the purpose of free speech, which liberates news reporters from government control. In the United States, the press may be free, but reporters do not ask politicians and the government the tough questions that need to be asked. On the other hand, the Soviet Union controlled all newspapers, TV channels, and book publishing. The Soviet government only told its citizens what the government wanted them to know.

The internet was A new technology that allowed anyone to become a writer. The internet has become the most versatile invention of the 20th century because anyone with access to a computer can become a press cheaply. However, some lawyers and judges have discovered ways to punish people who use the internet as a free press. For example, suppose a person creates a website or runs a TV commercial against a political opponent in Texas. In that case, this person may be violating a campaign finance law. Opponents could sue this person and pay high damages or even be subjected to criminal prosecution. Texas campaign law requires people to register with the state and disclose all financial contributors. Consequently, political organizations unhappy about negative campaign ads encourage and hound the Texas prosecutors to examine these cases for campaign law violations as a clever way to shut people up. Some Texas politicians utilize the campaign finance laws to quiet the Tea Party Movement,

The government has eroded the right to a peaceful assembly. Usually, when a political group becomes angry over an issue and wants politicians to pay attention, the group has a public protest. These protests make headlines that political leaders pay serious attention to. However, some political leaders do not like the message or the publicity, so they sic the police on them. Thus, the police have been aggressive toward the protesters, such as the Mexican protesters, who protested the new immigration laws in Los Angeles in 2007 [2], or the Occupy Wall Street protestors, who wanted to stop the corruption on Wall Street in 2011.

The government utilizes two methods to stop protests.

> **Method 1:** The government requires a permit. Hence, the government takes time to approve the permit or arrest the protesters if they do not get the necessary paperwork. Of course, the keyword is approval because the government can also decline permits, forcing citizens to undergo a lengthy appeal process. The government can create formidable roadblocks when it deems it necessary.

> **Method 2:** In 2012, President Obama passed a new law that allows the U.S. government to charge protestors with a felony if they protest near Secret Service agents. Ironically, when President Obama was 29 years old, he protested for minority rights at Harvard University in 1990. Leaders usually forget their roots as they climb up the leadership ladder.

The final assault of the First Amendment was the expansion of police powers after the terrorist attacks on September 11, 2001. President Bush and Congress passed the Patriot Act to broaden the federal government's surveillance and police powers. For example, the Federal Bureau of Investigation (FBI) could issue a National Security Letter and request information from any financial institution, library, insurance company, internet provider, or travel agency. The letter automatically comes with a lifetime gag order. Thus, a person cannot talk or write about it or confer with an attorney. The U.S. government can sentence a violator up to five years in prison [3].

A lifetime gag order creates two serious problems:

> **Problem 1:** A National Security Letter does not require approval from a judge. Thus, the FBI does not need probable cause.

> **Problem 2:** The FBI issued approximately 200,000 letters between 2003 and 2006 [3], which means the FBI is abusing its power.

Amendment II

"A well regulated Militia, being necessary to the security of a free State, the right of the people to keep and bear Arms, shall not be infringed" [1].

In the beginning, the United States did not have a large, full-time military because soldiers worked their jobs and farmed the land to support their families. Thus, the states needed access to soldiers, whom the state called up on short notice to protect people and towns from invaders and the Indians. (We did steal land from the Indians, so they have every right to be angry with the Europeans.) The state wanted their citizens to own their guns.

This Amendment clearly limits the federal government. If the federal government becomes too powerful, a state government could easily rebel because it has fast access to its armed population. If the federal government went too far, a potential bloody war could ensue. The United States lost more soldiers in the U.S. Civil War than in World Wars I and II combined because a civil war is the worst war a country can fight.

The current government has a problem with people owning guns, and it successfully placed barriers to gun ownership.

Common barriers include the following:

- ➤ **Barrier 1:** A person can own a gun but not fire it within city limits because of city ordinances. The government does not care about the circumstances.

- ➤ **Barrier 2:** In certain states, a person could be prosecuted if a burglar tries to break into the house and the owner shoots him. An owner can only go up one step to remove the threat. Of course, how could a person know what the threat level is as someone breaks into his or her home? The burglar could be unarmed or armed.

> **Barrier 3:** The government imposes another restriction—a person needs a special permit to carry a concealed weapon and must ask a government agency for permission to carry a firearm.

> **Barrier 4:** The government uses domestic violence as a popular means of gun control. A person loses their right to have a firearm if a court has convicted a person (i.e., male) of domestic violence or has issued a protective order against him. Of course, judges grant protective orders readily in some states as defendants cannot challenge them. If the defendants do not turn in all guns to the police, then the state can charge them with felonies for gun possession.

> **Barrier 5:** Felony convictions prevent gun ownership for the rest of a felon's life.

Why would a government want to limit gun ownership? Federal, state, and local governments tax, steal and confiscate property. The government rationalizes this behavior by labeling a person as a criminal or has broken an obscure law and must have his property and assets taken. It can be as simple as a person carrying too much cash, and the government steals the money by claiming this person is a drug dealer. If people are armed, the government has more difficulty expropriating property. Who in their right mind would want to be a government agent if every time the agent knocks on a door, the occupants shoot at the agent? This can become very expensive in terms of manpower and the potential loss of government agents.

Machiavelli (1520) summed it best in the *Art of War*. A republic with armed citizens has a longer life span than a Republic where the citizens are unarmed [4]. If the people are armed, then the government must be afraid of its people. If the government is armed, the people must fear the government. A leader can seize power and quickly establish a dictatorship if the people do not have weapons.

Amendment III

"No Soldier shall, in time of peace be quartered in any house, without the consent of the Owner, nor in time of war, but in a manner to be prescribed by law" [1].

The government did not violate this Amendment because the U.S. military receives tax dollars to house soldiers in barracks.

Amendment IV

"The right of the people to be secure in their persons, houses, papers, and effects, against unreasonable searches and seizures, shall not be violated, and no Warrants shall issue, but upon probable cause, supported by Oath or affirmation, and particularly describing the place to be searched, and the persons or things to be seized" [1].

The government easily circumvented this Amendment and used three methods, which include the following:

- ➢ **Method 1:** If the police want to search a house or vehicle, the police can lie and say anything to a judge or magistrate. Judges or magistrates usually sign the search warrants.

- ➢ **Method 2:** If police believe a person is armed or is destroying evidence, the police will crash through someone's door without a search warrant. This was an actual case in the federal district court in Texas. A person was showering and did not hear the police knocking on the door. Imagine the person's surprise to see a multitude of guns pointed at him as he stepped out of the shower. Federal courts deem this okay. Of course, to a person with common sense, how could the police ever know a person is armed or is destroying evidence? Police cannot read minds. Thus, the police have the power to kick in any door under these pretenses without the need for a warrant.

➢ **Method 3:** The Patriot Act expanded the federal government's powers. Federal agents can request information about a person using a National Security Letter, which was already discussed under the First Amendment.

State governments do not like this amendment. For example, the Texas Department of Transportation went after a homeowner who constructed a billboard on his property that stated the Fourth Amendment, 'Just say NO to police searches!' The Billboard also listed a telephone number with a pre-recorded message of the 4th Amendment. The Department of Transportation claimed the owner violated the Texas Highway Beautification Act when the State of Texas stepped up its campaign of "consent searches of vehicles on our highways." The homeowner won his case in court using "freedom of speech" from the First Amendment [5].

This homeowner was concerned the police were pulling over too many people and searching their cars. The homeowner did the right thing and posted our right about "unreasonable searches and seizures." If the police follow the rules and obtain a search warrant, they would need several hours. The judge must sign the search warrant and deliver the warrant to the person. These several hours could prevent police from pulling over a dozen more cars and searching them. Remember, time is money, and the police must keep writing tickets. However, Florida solved this problem by having a judge sit in a patrol car near a police checkpoint.

Police do not respect smart asses that say 'no' to an officer's request to search the vehicle. Of course, this could be dangerous in Texas, where police officers have their methods to deal with "difficult citizens."

Amendment V

"No person shall be held to answer for a capital, or otherwise infamous crime, unless on a presentment or indictment of a Grand Jury, except in cases arising in the land or naval forces, or in the Militia, when in actual service in time of War or public danger; nor shall any person be subject for the same offence to be twice put in jeopardy of life or limb; nor shall be compelled in any criminal case to be a witness against himself, nor be deprived of life, liberty, or property, without due process of law; nor shall private property be taken for public use, without just compensation" [1].

The government circumvented this Amendment. A grand jury approves severe charges against a person but does not state who serves on grand juries. In Harris County Courts (Houston, Texas), all judges choose the people who serve on grand juries. Only one judge selects a grand jury from voter registrations. We should not be surprised that retired police officers, retired prosecutors, and court employees are overrepresented on grand juries in Harris County. Could retired criminal justice system employees remain unbiased if their former colleagues have charged someone?

A grand jury investigated the Houston Crime Lab scandal and found no violations. The Grand jury had one Houston police officer as a member. However, the FBI shut down this same lab for numerous problems.

Prosecutors also shop around the court system and select a court with highly biased grand juries for weak court cases [6].

This Amendment also allows a government to seize property through eminent domain. Eminent domain is the power to condemn property and take it over without consent. Traditionally, the government only seized property for public projects, such as building a highway, expanding streets, building a new school, or expanding an airport. These public goods benefit society.

The key word is "just compensation." Property owners usually overvalue their property, while the government seizing it undervalues it. For example, a person owns a house worth $50,000, but he values it at $70,000, while the government wants to pay only $10,000. If a homeowner and government agency cannot agree on the compensation, this case would go to court, and a judge would decide the property value.

The first assault on private property started in the early 1970s, when Congress and the President signed the Endangered Species Act of 1973. This Law gave the federal government the power to halt land development if it harmed an endangered species or its habitat. The problem with this Law is that the federal government does not provide "just compensation."

For example, we buy a piece of land and want to build a house. Then the federal government finds an endangered bird living on our land and tells us to halt any construction. Now, the land drops in value because people do not want to hold land for the sake of having it. The government does not compensate the property owner for this loss. The federal government seized the land because it limited the activity a person could do. Congress knew the federal government's power would be severely limited if it had to compensate landowners when it[1] destroyed their land values. Similar laws protect wetlands. Many states impose laws restricting land development. For example, California has strict rules that prevent landowners from subdividing their property.

The final assault on property owners was the Supreme Court's decision, Kelo versus the City of New London. The court allows a government to seize land if it can collect more tax revenues. The government can seize property from one private owner and transfer it to another [7]. For example, a city government could use eminent domain to seize properties in a neighborhood and transfer the properties to a developer. Then a developer demolishes the homes and builds new condominiums or a shopping mall. New development brings in new property and sales taxes [8]. However, this power can have a chilling effect on private investment. Who would invest in a building or buy a condominium if a government seized the property again several years later? Consequently, the government has converted private property into a land lease from the government.

Amendment VI

"In all criminal prosecutions, the accused shall enjoy the right to a speedy and public trial, by an impartial jury of the State and district wherein the crime shall have been committed, which district shall

---

[1]Several laws are the Clean Water Act of 1972 and the Coastal Wetlands Planning, Protection and Restoration Act of 1990.

have been previously ascertained by law, and to be informed of the nature and cause of the accusation; to be confronted with the witnesses against him; to have compulsory process for obtaining witnesses in his favor, and to have the Assistance of Counsel for his defence" [1].

The Founding Fathers never specified the exact terms of this Amendment. For instance, what is a speedy trial? Does it mean the trial starts in one year, two years, or eight years? Consequently, prosecutors ensure a judge sets the defendant's bail too high so the defendant sits in jail. People do not enjoy sitting behind bars and will cave into a prosecutor's plea agreement even if they did not commit the crime. People sitting in jail for several months could lose their job, housing, and their standard of living. Hence, innocent people can be coerced into pleading guilty because it is the cheaper alternative.

Judges and prosecutors want to avoid jury trials because jury trials take time and are expensive. Prosecutors and defense attorneys spend significant time organizing the evidence, preparing witnesses, and filing paperwork with the court. Furthermore, jury trials are random events. In some cases, prosecutors had strong evidence, but the juries found the defendant not guilty. Other juries convicted defendants on circumstantial evidence.

Judges like to avoid jury trials. The court spends time summoning jurors, preparing the jury, and hearing the case, and a judge's docket becomes clogged with too many cases. If a problematic defendant demands a jury trial, prosecutors devise ingenious methods to force people to plead guilty and forgo their right to a jury trial. Examples include the following:

> ➢ **Example 1:** A defendant has two legitimate charges against him. A prosecutor invents and adds three additional bogus charges. The prosecutor will drop the three charges if the person pleads guilty to the original two. If a jury finds the person guilty of all five charges, this person will spend an extended vacation in prison.

> **Example 2:** Prosecutors can threaten to remove children or seize property unless the defendant accepts the prosecutor's plea agreement.

> **Example 3:** Prosecutors ask the judge to set a defendant's bail high. A person could be jailed for up to a year, waiting for his jury trial.

> **Example 4:** If the defendant posted bail, the person must appear before the judge every month. The court ensures the person appears, and the prosecutor asks for a continuance, i.e., more time. Subsequently, the judge resets the case for next month.

Resetting the case does two things. First, a person wasted his day to come to court, like taking a day off from work. Second, if that person brought his lawyer, he pays his lawyer to appear in court. If the court keeps resetting the case for two or more years, many defendants will give up and accept the plea bargain from the prosecutor. People cannot afford to bring an attorney to court month after month. Defense attorneys also do not mind because they come to court and are paid for doing nothing.

Judges have another problem. They can indirectly help prosecutors win court cases because they control the information that enters the court. In case we did not know, many judges were former prosecutors. The following cases illustrate these people are guilty without a doubt.

> Police catch an elderly woman smoking marijuana in her house.

> A person attacked another person with a weapon.

> A convicted felon fired a gun at another person. Thus, a felon possesses a firearm.

These are open and shut cases. However, would we change our minds if we had more information? Reread the cases.

- ➢ Police catch an elderly woman smoking marijuana in her house. She has severe glaucoma, and marijuana helps relieve the pain.

- ➢ A person attacked another person with a weapon. This other person molested the attacker's daughter, and the judge dismissed the child molestation case on a technicality.

- ➢ A convicted felon fired a gun at another person. This person was robbing the felon, and the felon grabbed the weapon, causing the gun to fire.

These cases are not fictional! They happened. For prosecutors to win these cases, they must hide this extraneous information. Of course, these people can appeal against a wrongful conviction. However, defendants usually cannot appeal a jury's decision; they can only appeal if a judge makes a mistake. In these cases, the violators did violate the letter of the law. Unfortunately, appeal judges do not consider extenuating circumstances, but juries would consider.

This Amendment allows defendants to bring witnesses in their favor. However, the criminal justice system must be honest because the police and prosecutors must disclose pertinent information to the defendant. What happens if a prosecutor or police does not turn over the evidence or names of all witnesses to the defense? Thus, defendants cannot request witnesses to appear on their behalf if they do not know their names. For instance, prosecutors always bring witnesses who claim the defendant committed the crime, while the defense brings witnesses who acquit the defendant. Police and prosecutors could withhold the name of a key witness that weakens a state's case.

This Amendment also requires criminal courts to supply attorneys for the poor, a Supreme Court ruling in Gideon versus Wainwright in 1963. Thus, all states must counsel poor defendants for severe misdemeanors and felonies. Unfortunately, many states ensure public defenders earn the lowest salaries, are overburdened with heavy caseloads, and provide no financial assistance for expert witnesses. Consequently, public defender offices have trouble retaining experienced attorneys, have high turnover rates, and have difficulty recruiting reasonable attorneys [9, 10]. Prosecutors also make the same claims for their offices but earn higher salaries than public defenders.

The State of Texas provided one attorney who slept during a death-penalty trial. The State of Texas claimed the "death sentence should be upheld because a sleeping lawyer is no different from a lawyer, who is intoxicated, under the influence of drugs, suffering from Alzheimer's disease or having a psychotic break." After a lengthy appeals court battle, the defendant was granted a new trial [11].

States vary widely in how they fund public defenders. States use the following standard methods:

> **Method 1:** Court provides legal counsel [9]. A judge hires a private attorney to represent poor defendants who stand before the judge. In this case, do the private attorneys represent the defendants or work for the judges? Is justice served, or do the judges want to clear their dockets with guilty pleas?

> **Method 2:** The court uses a public defender's office that sends an attorney to represent poor defendants. Public defender's offices receive funding from the county and state governments [9].

Amendment VII

"In suits at common law, where the value in controversy shall exceed twenty dollars, the right of trial by jury shall be preserved, and no fact tried by a jury, shall be otherwise reexamined in any Court of the United States, than according to the rules of the common law" [1].

Local, state, and federal governments have rewritten laws removing jury trials. For example, the State of Texas changed its rules for red-light cameras, changing a traffic violation from a criminal offense to a civil one. Thus, city governments can choose whether to provide jury trials.

The City of Houston currently has 70 red-light cameras, and some members of the city council want to expand the number to 200. Mayor Bill White claimed that "cameras raise awareness about red-light safety and free up officers to patrol neighborhoods" [12].

The state changed the law for red cameras to grab more money from local governments. In 2008, the red cameras generated 387,000 citations. A violation costs $75, which equals $29 million in revenue if all violators pay the fine. If 10% of the violators requested a jury trial, the violators would flood the court system with new cases.

The government uses red-light cameras to increase public safety. However, the number of collisions at intersections with red-light cameras doubled since they were installed. If the City of Houston is concerned about public safety, the red-light cameras should be removed [13]. This Amendment clearly states all citizens can request a jury trial if the fine exceeds $20. Unfortunately, the government exempts itself from the law, while the public must comply.

Citizens and businesses do not get jury trials in many cases. Many states set up special courts to decide these cases, such as the following:

> **Case 1:** Defendants do not get jury trials for tax code violations in many states.

> **Case 2:** Defendants do not get jury trials for civil infractions, which include traffic tickets, housing code violations, and pet violations.

> **Case 3:** Juries do not hear court cases involving children.

> **Case 4:** President Obama signed the National Defense Authorization Act. If the government labels a U.S. citizen a

terrorist, he or she can be detained indefinitely without a jury trial. Unfortunately, one definition of a terrorist is a person who quotes the Bill of Rights or reads passages from the U.S. Constitution.

Many heart-wrenching stories come from courts that deny jury trials because jury trials impose an immense check on the government.

Amendment VIII

"Excessive bail shall not be required, nor excessive fines imposed, nor cruel and unusual punishments inflicted" [1].

The legal system has abused this Amendment's "cruel and unusual punishment" clause. Cruel and unusual punishment is a judgment call. The United States reserves the death penalty for treason and premeditated murder. However, the U.S. Supreme Court ruled the death penalty unconstitutional in 1972 but reinstituted it in 1976. The government uses the death penalty to deter crime because a violator pays the ultimate price for murder or treason. Furthermore, some people are psychopaths and inherently evil. Society would be better if the state removed these people permanently.

Here is where the legal system gets crazy. Federal and several state governments use lethal injections to execute prisoners because they consider this a more humane method. However, firing squads, hangings, and electric chairs constitute cruel and unusual punishment. All these methods have one common theme. They induce death to the prisoner. Death is death! Does it matter if it takes 10 seconds to kill a prisoner or 2 minutes? Is one method of death more humane than another method?

States could save money by incarcerating a person for the rest of his life than pay for the legal appeals of the death penalty. Unfortunately, the attorneys use the death penalty as a source of employment. For instance, the most ridiculous case involves the appeals of Richard Cooey. A judge sentenced Richard to die in 2008 because he murdered two college students. Richard claimed he was too fat to die, and the executioners would have trouble finding his veins to administer the injection. Consequently, lethal injection, in his case, would constitute cruel and unusual punishment. (Richard never claimed he was innocent.) This is not made up! U.S. Supreme Court denied his appeal [14]. For this case to appear before the U.S. Supreme Court and Ohio Supreme Court, lawyers filed paperwork and generated time on this case. Who paid for this time? Unfortunately, the taxpayers pay for the indigent defendants.

Funding for the death penalty cases should go towards the trial. Judges and lawyers ensure that defendants receive fair trials and have a fair chance to defend themselves. Unfortunately, many state and county courts push convictions through for poor defendants with no concern for their rights.

The criminal justice system has become sensitive to particular crimes after the terrorist attacks on the United States on September 11, 2001, and several prominent school shootings. For example, on the way to school, a student called a rival bus and threatened to open fire on them. Although this was a tasteless joke, a judge sentenced a 17-year-old kid to eight years in prison for making terroristic death threats in Tyler, Texas. The kid had no means and no weapons. The judge stated, "the times we live in" [15]. This kid should be punished, but does this crime necessitate eight years in prison?

Hate crimes should constitute cruel and unusual punishment because hate crimes skew efficient punishment systems. An efficient punishment system is one in which minor crimes warrant less severe sentences than serious crimes. Thus, the punishment matches the severity of the crime. Table 1 shows an efficient punishment scale. An inefficient punishment system would be a criminal who gets ten years for murder but the death penalty for attempted murder. If all murderers know this, then they kill the victim.

Hate crimes add a dimension of capriciousness and unfairness to the justice system—first, the same crime results in different penalties. If two white men had fought, they would get the regular penalties. If two men had fought, and one is a minority while the other is white, then the court must punish the whites more severely.

Second, prosecutors determine whether to charge a defendant with a hate crime. In some cases, the prosecutor charges defendants with a hate crime; in others, he does not. Third, more defendants may challenge the charges and request jury trials because a hate crime conviction adds more time to a person's sentence. Consequently, the defendant could challenge the charges. Finally, courts already have trouble determining whether a defendant is guilty. A hate crime requires the court to get into the defendant's head, which makes court cases more complicated.

Table 1: Efficient Punishment System

Crime	Punishment
(1) Assault without a weapon, drinking while intoxicated, etc.	Fines, probation, and/or time in jail
(2) Assault with a weapon	Some prison time
(3) Rape, attempted murder, and child molestation	Decades in prison
(4) Murder	Death penalty or life in prison

Criminal records constitute "cruel and unusual punishment." Before computers, if employers wanted to check an applicant's background, they would go to the courthouse to search the court records. Consequently, most people did not check criminal records. If a person moves to a new state, they would start with a clean slate because employers cannot check criminal records in other states. Cases exist where a convict broke out of prison and became a schoolteacher in another state. Now, everyone has potential access to criminal records through the Internet from all 50 states.

Problems with a criminal record include the following:

> **Problem 1:** A criminal record exists forever, so a conviction follows a person throughout his life. Punishment for minor crimes should have a stopping point. For severe crimes, the person would sit in prison for a long time so that a criminal record would be irrelevant.

> **Problem 2:** A criminal record for a person may exist in a court's database, the state's database, usually administered

by the state police, and the FBI's database. Furthermore, the FBI connects all police and state criminal databases as one extensive database for the whole United States and Canada, which the FBI calls the National Crime Information Center (NCIC). What happens if a person has a mistake in their criminal record? What would happen if the wrong name was recorded in a database? This has happened! People were denied jobs because a background check revealed a felony conviction that was a mistake. Unfortunately, the burden of the proof falls upon the person with the false record. He must hire an attorney and legally challenge the record, which could be expensive and time-consuming.

➢ **Problem 3:** Many states release arrest records. If police falsely arrest a person and the case never goes to trial, the arrest record remains. Would an employer hire someone who was arrested for "assault with a weapon," although the state dropped the charges?

➢ **Problem 4:** Vindictive people have falsely accused victims of crimes they did not commit. In other cases, police and prosecutors were overly aggressive. For example, a person was arrested for barking at a police dog. Unfortunately, his criminal record contains the charge of" assaulting a police officer." His criminal record would never give details, such as the "defendant barked at a police dog."

Our Founding Fathers did not intend to use court records to shackle a person for the rest of his life. The public can view court records because they keep the judges honest. If a judge makes a wrong decision, and the public knows it, it could lead to a public outcry.

Amendment IX

"The enumeration in the Constitution, of certain rights, shall not be construed to deny or disparage others retained by the people" [1].

No problems were found with this Amendment.

Amendment X

"The powers not delegated to the United States by the Constitution, nor prohibited by it to the States, are reserved to the States respectively, or to the people" [1].

Although this Amendment recognizes state power, the federal government uses three ingenious methods to circumvent this Amendment.

> **Method 1:** The federal government broadly interprets the powers in the Constitution and maintains a multitude of federal bureaucracies. Bureaucracies impose numerous unfunded mandates on state and local governments.

> **Method 2:** The federal government has the right to regulate interstate commerce.

> **Method 3:** The federal government funds various projects, and this money comes with a long list of conditions.

U.S. Congress and the President founded powerful federal bureaucracies. For example, the U.S. government created the Environmental Protection Agency (EPA) in 1970 to protect the environment. If we read the U.S. Constitution, no language can be construed that gives the federal government this vast power to create a bureaucracy to protect the environment. Unfortunately, the EPA actively enforces the environmental regulations.

EPA imposes standards on people, businesses, and state and local governments. For example, the EPA ordered water utility companies in central Oklahoma to lower the arsenic levels. However, the mandates have two problems: First, the EPA does not pay the cost of its ruling. It dictates the rules that people, businesses, and local governments must follow. Second, the EPA did not give people in central Oklahoma the right to determine which arsenic level they would be happy with. However, they will pay higher local taxes or greater water bills so that the water treatment facilities comply with the EPA's ruling.

The federal government has the right to regulate interstate commerce. What is interstate commerce? A business makes something that residents in another state consume. Thus, a company can produce anything potentially involved in interstate commerce. Traditional examples include the following:

> **Example 1:** A grid of wires connects electric power plants and their customers. This grid crosses state lines, and hence, the federal government regulates this whole industry. One state, Texas, did not connect to the national grid so that Texas could escape from the federal regulators.

> **Example 2:** Airplanes fly between airports located in different states. Thus, the federal government regulates the airline industry. When Southwest Airlines first started, it only flew airplanes within Texas and escaped from the federal regulators. Southwest had a cost advantage and grew fast before going national.

> **Example 3:** The federal government regulates the trucking industry because trucks transport freight from one state to another.

> **Example 4:** The federal government regulates the food and pharmaceutical industries because products cross state lines.

> **Example 5:** President Obama used the interstate commerce clause to pass his healthcare plan. The federal government wants all U.S. citizens living within the U.S. to purchase healthcare insurance. Obamacare was challenged in court in 2012, but the courts did not find it unconstitutional.

A recent Supreme Court case, Gonzales versus Raich, re-asserts the federal government's power to regulate interstate commerce. The state of California allows residents to smoke marijuana for medicinal purposes because marijuana helps people with glaucoma and eases pain from multiple sclerosis and cancer. However, the federal government still views marijuana use as a crime. A person sued the federal government to stop its intrusion over a state's right. Consequently, the Supreme Court ruled marijuana use in interstate commerce, and the federal government has the right to pursue violators [16]. Thus, the federal government can potentially regulate all industries and businesses.

For the last method, the federal government controls states by controlling the money. The federal government funds various projects and uses this funding to dictate laws and conditions. For example, the federal government imposed the legal drinking age 21 on all the states. Nowhere in the U.S. Constitution does the federal government have the legal authority to set the legal drinking age. No words in the Constitution could be interpreted broadly enough to give Congress the power to pass such a law. However, the federal government threatened to reduce funding for highway projects in several states if these states did not raise the legal drinking age from 18 to 21. People can marry, enter contracts, own property, or be sent to another country to die in a war at the age of 18, but they cannot drink alcohol until they have reached age 21.

Conclusion

We always had problems that plagued our justice system. Before the 1960s, the judicial system was small and had little interaction with its citizens. Thus, injustice would be a rare event, but it did happen. Initially, courts sustained slavery and enforced discrimination against women during the 19th century. Nowadays, courts from the city level to the U.S. Supreme Court rule over everything. Judges invaded families, schools, neighborhoods, and businesses. Consequently, injustices occur frequently as judges shove their hands into everything.

Judges became social crusaders. They believed they had the right to regulate all of society's bad behavior. They overextended the law to achieve their goals. This caused a problem with the Bill of Rights because this document limits the government's power. Consequently, judges allowed the government to circumvent it through court rulings.

Before the 1970s, the following were not crimes:

➤ People could smoke cigarettes freely.

➤ Parents and school officials could spank children.

➤ Some families are violent and fight. Police would break up the fights and force some family members to leave.

➤ One parent would take (or kidnap) the children if they disagreed with a custody agreement.

➤ People used drugs and alcohol openly. Parents could throw a keg party for a child who graduated from high school. High-school students could smoke reefer during lunch on school property.

All these activities have become illegal. The criminal justice system expanded to go after people committing these new crimes. Furthermore, judges enforce the laws that indirectly target families. Families have members who work and are a source of wealth and income. Thus, family members are afraid to go to jail or be incarcerated. They will cave into the state's demands, pay fines and fees, and not challenge the state. On the other hand, the state has to expend resources to go after real criminals, and the criminals have little resources to reimburse the state.

Courts and government believe they are making the United States a better place to live. People, who have been around for several decades, know this is a bunch of crap. Ronald Reagan said it best, "Are we better off now than we were ten years ago?"

References

[1] The Bill of Rights. 1791. National Archives Experience. Available at http://www.archives.gov/national_archives_experience/bill_of_rights_trans cript.html (access date: 12/24/08).

[2] Associated Press. May 4, 2007. "Police chief 'not happy' with LAPD immigration clash." *USA Today*. Available at http://www.usatoday.com/news/nation/2007-04-26-LAPD-immigration-rally_N.htm (access date 01/09/09).

[3] Zetter, Kim. August 10, 2010. "'John Doe' Who Fought FBI Spying Freed From Gag Order After 6 Years." *Wired*. Available from www.wired.com.

[4] Machiavelli, Niccolo. 1520. The Seven Books on the Art of War.

[5] Blumner, Robyn E. August 1, 1999. "What's this man's sign? Try the Fourth Amendment." *St. Petersburg Times*.

[6] McVicker, Steve. November 13, 2004. "Are judges taking a narrow view of justice?" *Houston Chronicle*.

[7] Associated Press. June 23, 2005. "Homes may be 'taken' for private projects." *MSNBC*.

[8] Jones, Tim. November 16, 2003. "Private property gets condemned for profit." *Chicago Tribune*.

[9] Parker, Laura. September 29, 2005. "8 years in a Louisiana jail, but he never went to trial." *USA Today*.

[10] Patrick, Robert. March 6, 2005. "Public lawyers face low pay, high turnover." *St. Louis Post-Dispatch*.

[11] The Justice Project. August 14, 2001. "Texas Death Row Defendant With Sleeping Lawyer Deserves New Trial, Rules Full Fifth Circuit Court." Available from www.thejusticeproject.com

[12] Houston Politics. June 11, 2008. "Rodriguez: More red-light cameras = more officers." *Houston Chronicle*.

[13] Olson, Bradley. December 29, 2008. "Study: Wrecks increase at red-light cameras sites." *Houston Chronicle*.

[14] Kinney, Terry. October 14, 2008. "Inmate who says he's too fat to die to be executed." *South Bend Tribune*.

[15] Associated Press. June 7, 2008. "Student, 17, gets 8 years in prison for phone threat." *Houston Chronicle*.

[16] Mears, Bill. June 7, 2005. "Supreme Court allows prosecution of medical marijuana." *CNN*.

8. Repeating History – The Roman Empire

"When thou art at Rome, do as they do at Rome."
-Miguel de Cervantes

The ancient Roman Empire and the United States share many characteristics. The Roman Empire dominated the civilized world between the eighth century B.C. and the fifth century A.D., whereas the United States dominated the 20th century and early 21st century. We study the Roman Empire to illustrate the life-cycle theory of a legal system because many empires experience a life cycle. Every life cycle stage has prominent characteristics, and we compare the characteristics of the Roman Empire to those of the United States.

The evolution of a legal system can be delineated into several key stages. It begins with the formation of a new society that establishes a strong legal system, fostering a culture of hard work, strong private property rights, and free enterprise. This environment encourages the growth of businesses, which in turn, generate wealth by catering to consumer needs. The role of the government in this stage is to set the rules of the game and finance itself through tax collection.

As wealth and incomes increase, the government collects large tax revenue flows, giving birth to government bureaucracies. Eventually, bureaucracies increase in size of their own volition and always need taxes to sustain this growth. Eventually, these bureaucracies become so large that they destroy free markets. They pass complicated, convoluted rules and regulations and impose numerous taxes until society no longer has free enterprise.

When a legal system reaches a stage of excessive taxes, regulations, and large bureaucracies, it can lead to societal stagnation. Businesses may flee or go bankrupt, wealth and incomes fall, and unemployment rises. Despite these signs of trouble, the bureaucracies continue to expand and raise taxes, further burdening an already stagnant economy. Ultimately, this can lead to the collapse of a once prosperous country, transforming it into a third-world banana republic.

The Roman Empire went through this life-cycle of a legal system. Historians define two eras: the Roman Republic and the

Roman Empire. In the beginning, the Roman Republic started as a democracy and grew incredibly. As a democracy, the government granted citizens legal rights, including voting rights. As the Roman Republic approached its apogee and its military dominated the world, the Republic transformed into the Roman Empire that an emperor controlled. The emperor was a dictator who controlled all government institutions and people. Towards the end of the Roman Empire, the empire evolved into a totalitarian state, with the Roman Empire having absolute power until the Western Roman Empire collapsed in the fifth century. At the same time, the Eastern Roman Empire, the Byzantium Empire, survived until the 15th century.

The Roman Republic Rises

Kings ruled Rome for the first 200 years until the aristocrats expelled the last king and established a republic. The Republic was a representative government, or in other words, a democracy controlled by a Senate. Only aristocrats, called patricians, could sit in the Senate, and the Senate controlled the government machinery.

Aristocrats strongly distrusted powerful kings, and they decentralized the power of the government. Furthermore, the Romans published Roman law on twelve tablets, and the laws emphasized that "all free citizens had their rights to fair justice guaranteed" [1]. Early Romans also gave its citizens the right to vote and hold public office, whereas the Roman government defined citizens in narrow terms. Citizens were free adult males who owned weapons, and the weapon requirement was necessary so the government could call people to serve in the military [2]. Finally, Roman laws were shaped by actual court cases and common sense. Romans had a standard law legal system that emphasized individual rights and the private ownership of property.

It's like history repeating itself-the United States Founding Fathers, much like their Roman counterparts, established the United States as a republic after defeating the British army. Both groups shared a deep distrust of kings and created decentralized governments. Our cherished rights, such as the right to vote and hold public office, echo those of the Romans. Of course, these rights were initially restricted to white, adult males who owned property. Just like the Romans, Americans adopted the British Common Law system, which is pro-business, allows court cases to shape the law, and builds a strong foundation for private property rights.

The United States and ancient Rome absorbed the cultures of other countries. For example, the Romans imported the Etruscan's artistic and architectural styles, which included the Roman's trademark – the arch. Moreover, Rome absorbed their religious, legal, and political ideas from other cultures and the gladiators, who fought to their deaths [3]. Likewise, the United States absorbs the culture, ideas, and people from different countries as the United States becomes a melting pot of all the world's cultures and people. We take the best from the world and assimilate it into our culture.

The United States and Romans integrated the conquered lands and people into their country. The Romans granted legal rights and citizenship to the conquered people and introduced them to the Latin language, Roman law, and customs [4, 5]. The Romans did expropriate lands and booty from the conquered countries but were ingenious when conquering them. Once the Roman Republic integrated the conquered nations, these countries could share the spoils with Rome if Rome conquered new territories [6]. Likewise, the United States expanded its boundaries by annexing new states to the Union. As the United States expanded westward across the Great Plains, it allowed new states to form and become equal members with the other older states. New states could send senators and representatives to Congress and have their citizens elected to the highest levels of government.

Many countries form colonies if they expand beyond their borders. Leaders do not possess the foresight to integrate conquered lands and people. An empire usually extracts as much wealth and resources as it can from a colony and treats the conquered people as inferior and subhuman. Over time, the poor treatment causes tension, leading to revolts and uprisings. Then the empire finances a military to squash the revolts and restore order. Eventually, the empire must withdraw and pull out if the military costs become too high.

The United States was a colony of the British Empire, and the British spent large sums of money on armies to protect the Midwest territories from the French and Indians. The British crown wanted the American colonies to help pay the military costs through new taxes, but the American colonies had no representation in England. Colonists were second-class citizens. Eventually, Americans revolted and broke away from the British Empire.

The United States and the Roman Republic both connected their citizens and cities with a massive infrastructure. The Romans, in particular, left a lasting legacy with their aqueducts, baths, bridges, and roads. Even after 2,000 years, some of this infrastructure still exists and is being used in the 21st century. For example, several aqueducts built in the Augustan Age still transport water to Rome. The people in southern France still use the aqueduct, Pont du Gard. The Spanish still cross a Roman bridge in Alcantara. This enduring legacy is a testament to the ingenuity and engineering prowess of the ancient Romans.

A good infrastructure allows a strong economy to form. A large, efficient infrastructure lets different regions specialize in products and services and sell them to consumers anywhere within the country. Businesses can transport Idaho potatoes, Michigan automobiles, Texas crude oil, and Florida oranges to any place cheaply within the United States or the world. Consequently, trade flourishes as businesses rush products from one side of a country to the other side.

Birth of the Roman Empire

Towards the end of the Republic, the Roman Republic fell into decline while politics dissolved into chaos. The Republic fragmented into quarrying groups [10], and two civil wars disrupted it with an explosion of violence [11]. Many Senators became fearful of powerful and popular generals like Caesar and Pompey because they could take advantage of the political chaos and seize control of the government.

Caesar was popular with the people because he was a brilliant general, a war hero, had the gift of rhetoric, and was born into a noble class. Some Senators feared Caesar and tried to turn Pompey and Caesar against each other. Other Senators wanted Caesar to relinquish control of his army so that they could file corruption charges against him, removing him from power by using the Roman court system. However, Caesar rebelled against the government using his army and defeated Pompey's army. Subsequently, Caesar gained control of the Roman government, but his long-term plans were cut short when several conservatives of the Senate assassinated Caesar [12].

The Roman government fell into disarray as its fiscal health was declining fast. Rome accumulated a large debt, experienced declining revenues, and issued new coins [13]. Top leaders could not control the government budget and hiked taxes to cover budget shortfalls. The government taxed anything with a name. The government imposed head taxes on free men and slaves. The government levied corn, soldiers, arms, equipment, and transport taxes. The Roman government even levied taxes on columns and doors [14]. As poverty spread throughout the Republic, the people fled from the poverty in the countryside and moved to Rome. They remained idle, seeking free corn and public aid [15].

The Senate was considered entirely corrupt. Senators would lend money at exorbitant interest rates to people who lived in the provinces so they could buy luxury items or pay taxes. Provinces were conquered Roman territories located outside of Italy. Senators would also receive bribes from tax farming, where bidders paid bribes to collect taxes in the provinces [16]. Some Senators would serve one-year terms as governors of the provinces. During that one year, the governors extorted as much property and wealth as possible through taxes. In some towns and regions, the people were impoverished and could not pay poll taxes [17].

In the final days of the Republic, politicians won elections by bribery, corruption, and violence [18]. Senators and other top government officials bribed judges and juries. In one instance, the Roman government charged the Governor of Sicily with mismanagement because he plundered the wealth of his province. He would use the first year's profits for his defense attorney; the second year's profits were used to pay the jury, and he pocketed the third year's profits [19]. Nevertheless, the prosecutor was Cicero, who was one of the greatest lawyers of the Roman Republic. The governor fled into exile because he knew he would not win his court case against the powerful Cicero.

Cicero was a young attorney, philosopher, and one of the most brilliant orators to rise out of the Roman Republic. Cicero was born from equestrian stock but rose to the consulship. An equestrian comes from the lower class of aristocrats, while the upper class is the patricians. A patrician could only hold the consulship with a few exceptions. Cicero firmly believed in the Roman Republic and tried to prevent the government's transformation into a dictatorship [20].

The rich became more ostentatious towards the end of the Roman Republic, and the number of rich was so few that Cicero remarked, "less than 1,000 men in Rome were wealthy" [21]. The affluent or aristocrats were few but controlled the machinery of the Roman government [22]. The wealthiest Roman citizens ostentatiously displayed their wealth and used it to bribe elections and juries [23].

Early in the Republic, families own small plots of land to grow crops. Then families could sell their surplus crops in the markets. Toward the end of the Republic, nobles bought or expropriated the small plots and public lands and consolidated them into large estates. Subsequently, the nobles pushed the families off the land and used the property-less tenants and slaves to cultivate the land. For instance, the rich stole a poor man's land if he served too long in the Roman military [24]. Top officials used another method. They confiscate a person's property when assessing a fine or penalty [25].

The Romans grew tired of the political chaos and violence. They were fed up with the pirates roaming the seas and thieves strolling the countryside. They yearned for peace and wanted law and order [26]. One person rose to meet the challenge: Gaius Julias Caesar Octavianus, otherwise known as Augustus. Augustus was Caesar's grandnephew and inherited 3/4 of Caesar's wealth. Augustus used his wealth to raise an army and crushed the armies of the conservatives, who murdered Caesar. He also assassinated Cicero [27].

Augustus was a dictator who became Rome's first emperor. Many consider Augustus one of the greatest leaders of the ancient world because he restored law and order and established a new framework of government [28]. People of the Roman Empire suffered less from extortion and had a more friendly form of government. Augustus even tried to address the immorality of his times [29] and allowed the autonomy of local governments [30].

Augustus's reforms brought peace and prosperity to the Roman Empire for the next 200 years. "More people could enjoy the fruits of prosperity than was possible again for the following 1,500 years" [31]. The Augustan Age led to a massive construction spree where large public projects were constructed, such as amphitheaters, aqueducts, bathhouses, coliseums, and temples. The pollution record in the polar icecaps captured this construction boom and the sharp decline that occurred in the third century A.D. [32].

New cities were founded while the older cities proliferated. Trade flourished within and outside the Roman Empire, which established trade routes with Arabia, India, and China [33]. Furthermore, the arts and letters prospered under the Augustan Age. Several cities instituted public education that taught reading, writing, and arithmetic [34].

The Roman legal system changed gradually as Roman emperors consolidated their power. Towards the end of the Roman Empire, the Roman government evolved into a total dictatorship, with the emperor controlling every aspect of the state and Roman society [35].

We argue that the United States is developing in a similar fashion. Federal, state, and local governments are passing laws that boost the government's power while restricting people's rights. The size, scope, and mission of government have become an intrusive, large sector of the U.S. economy. Consequently, a huge government with a strong military can give birth to an empire as strong authoritarian rulers replace the democratic legal system.

The Empire Goes into Decline

The Roman Empire declined during its last three centuries. Each Emperor assumed more control over society and raised taxes to finance a growing, bloated government bureaucracy. The Roman government kept hiking taxes to pay for three institutions, which include the following:

- ➤ Rome financed its army and navy, which was the biggest expense in the Emperor's budget. Over time, emperors bought the troops' loyalty with cash [36].

- ➤ The government bureaucracies became more extensive, more complicated, and more expensive.

- ➤ The government provided social welfare to feed the poor in Rome. The emperors provided free bread, Spanish olive oil, salt, and pork to Roman citizens and imposed price controls on wine [37].

The Roman government had trouble financing these activities as Rome's prosperity worsened. The Roman government raised taxes to high and oppressive levels [38]. Written history does not contain enough information about the level and oppressiveness of the Roman tax system. Still, historians have several accounts of the high taxes at the end of the Roman Empire. For example, Egyptian leaders complained to Rome about taxes because people fled the villages, escaping from the tax collectors. If someone defaulted on his tax payments and fled, the tax collectors would beat the person's family and relatives and subject them to other types of punishment. Family and relatives would either pay the taxes or tell the tax collector the tax evader's hiding place. Tax collectors invented new forms of executions for tax defaulters. If no family or relatives were left, the tax collectors would punish the tax evader's neighbors or seek revenge on whole villages [39]. The Roman tax system destroyed the taxpayers [40]. (You probably thought dealing with the Internal Revenue Service was terrible, but it could be much worse).

The government can finance a large government by printing money to cover its spending. Although the Roman government minted coins from silver, the emperors debased the coins to create more money. When the silver coins were returned to the government, they melted them down and mixed them with cheap metals like copper. Then the government increased the money supply by making more coins with less silver. At the beginning of the Empire, coins were almost pure silver. Towards the end of the Empire, coins contained a speck of silver. The rapid increase in the money supply caused rampant inflation and weakened the currency. Heavy taxation and a weak currency put Rome's financial system in decline. Lastly, the high inflation drove food from the markets [38].

The Roman local governments had trouble balancing their budgets. They spent more than what they collected in taxes. Other things changed as well. At the end of the Roman Empire, the Emperor eliminated the autonomy of local government. The Emperor interfered with local government administration and imposed rules and mandates on local governments. City councils collected taxes, enlisted military recruits, and enforced the Emperor's orders [38, 41].

The Roman society evolved into a police state with an all-powerful central government [42]. Peasants became tied to the farmlands, making free movement impossible. Peasants cultivated the fields and became recruits for the Roman army when the Emperor needed soldiers [43]. The Roman emperors even established secret police, who would trick people into saying bad words about the Emperor so the police could arrest and execute them [44].

The population started decreasing in the second century A.D., along with declining production. Fewer people have a lower demand for goods and services because they buy fewer homes, food, and other products and services. Over time, industries contract. A smaller population also places pressure on the armed forces [38]. Furthermore, technological improvements halted [38] because, under an oppressive state, men no longer create fresh, original ideas [45].

Some scholars believe the Roman Empire should have collapsed in the third century A.D., but two emperors, Gallienus and Diocletian, reformed it. Emperor Gallienus reformed and restructured the Roman army and navy and introduced the cavalry. A cavalry consisted of armed soldiers mounted on horses, becoming mobile and an efficient striking force. Emperor Gallienus could suppress internal rebellion quickly or drive out the invaders.

However, the Roman government paid greater costs to feed both soldiers and their horses [46].

Emperor Diocletian reorganized the whole Roman Empire. He reformed and restructured the Roman army, navy, and the tax system. He proclaimed, "No man shall possess any property that is tax exempt" [43]. Diocletian divided the provinces into smaller units and created a new class of bureaucrats who regulated the Empire, causing further financial burden. An orator once remarked that bureaucrats are "more numerous than flies on sheep in the springtime" [47].

Diocletian further split the Roman Empire into the Western and Eastern Empires. Thus, the emperors retained tighter control over the provinces, which reduced internal strife and conflicts between the provinces and Rome. Diocletian usurped control and freedom from local governments, binding them to an all-powerful emperor. Unfortunately, the growth in bureaucracies isolated and buffered an emperor from his people. Finally, each person inherited their parents' social class, completely freezing social mobility [48].

By the third century A.D., the Empire blamed Christians for its economic hardships. The Roman government executed any church member [49]. Another reformer, Constantine the Great, proclaimed religious tolerance in 313. Emperor Constantine became the first Christian Emperor and switched the state's religion to Christianity.

Restructuring can shock a legal system and temporarily restore bureaucracies to function correctly. However, the emperors kept increasing the size of the government, and the benefits of restructuring could be short-lived [41]. Unfortunately, the increase in an emperor's power led to arbitrary rules, graft, favoritism, and corruption at all levels of government.

The government became larger, more oppressive, and more inefficient towards the end of the Roman Empire. Restructuring of the Empire from Gallienus and Diocletian evaporated because the Roman Empire showed signs of collapse in the fifth century. For instance, Rome possessed one characteristic of a banana republic. The army routinely murdered the emperor and then appointed another [50]. Technically, Roman law forbade an emperor to station an army in Rome. However, Roman emperors created armed guards called the Praetorian Guard that routinely assassinated an emperor and appointed another.

With the constantly changing Roman leadership coupled with severe financial troubles, people along the northern frontiers frequently rebelled against the Roman government [51]. The Roman Empire fell into barbarism as the dividing line between civilization and savagery disappeared. No wonder why the Germans could raid the Empire quickly [52].

Conclusion

Delving into the complexities of Rome's history, a civilization that collapsed over 15 centuries ago, is a fascinating and significant topic. The author's interpretation of events, particularly the emphasis on a growing government and its hunger for tax revenue, is a testament to the parallels we can draw between ancient Rome and modern societies. This is the essence of a historian's job-to use inference and deductions to connect the dots in a story where many details and facts are missing.

Rome started with a great legal system, and over time, the Roman government, through an emperor, took complete control over its economy. We see the same pattern in the United States. The United States started with a great legal system, but now, the government at all levels exerts its influence over all aspects of the economy. We differ from Rome only because the rate of change occurs at a faster pace.

Technological progress has played a pivotal role in shaping the life cycle of legal systems. Consider the Roman Republic, which lasted 500 years before transforming into a dictatorship, and the Western Roman Empire, which lasted another 500 years before collapsing under an oppressive government. In contrast, the Soviet Union lasted about 70 years, and the United States, with its rapid technological advancements, is showing signs of strain after just 200 years. This insight into the impact of technology on legal systems is both enlightening and informative.

Technology allows a government to control its population and rapidly change the legal system. Modern states can easily squash troublemakers and quickly execute or imprison them. Governments can use Global Positioning Satellites, vast computer databases, and a large military to exert a tight grip over their people and citizens.

Ancient Rome experienced another trend—a declining population. Economic prosperity usually slows down a country's population growth rate. People want to accumulate assets and wealth and obtain an education. As the level of society's wealth increases, people need a longer time to accumulate this wealth. The antithesis of wealth is children. Unfortunately, bearing and raising children are time-intensive and hamper the accumulation of wealth. Therefore, many couples have no kids or few kids in wealthy societies.

European countries like Germany have almost no growth in population, while the United States has little population growth from immigration. Over time, fewer people mean fewer consumers. All industries experience a gradual decline in demand for their products. Furthermore, all units of government have fewer people to regulate and control. That becomes the crux. The government rarely contracts its size, scope, and mission. If the government maintains its original size or expands, a smaller population means people pay larger tax bills. Then higher taxes coupled with more regulations over time become so burdensome that it causes the economy to fail.

The declining population is impacting several regions of the United States—for example, many cities in the State of New York experience declining populations. As the residents flee, the size of municipal governments rarely contracts. Instead, they devise new and greater taxes, further driving businesses and people from the State of New York.

References

[1] Starr, Chester G. 1971. *The Ancient Romans*. New York, NY: Oxford University Press, pp. 12-16.
[2] Nardo, Don. 2002. *The Rise of the Roman Empire*. San Diego, CA: Greenhaven Press, Inc., p. 23.
[3] Ibid, p. 22.
[4] Ibid, p. 25.
[5] Starr, Chester G. 1971. *The Ancient Romans*. New York, NY: Oxford University Press, p. 21.

[6] Crawford, Michael. 1978. *The Roman Republic*. Cambridge, MA: Harvard University Press, p. 46.
[7] Grant, Michael. 1999. *The Collapse and Recovery of the Roman Empire*. London and New York, NY: Routledge, p. 68.
[8] Starr, Chester G. 1971. *The Ancient Romans*. New York, NY: Oxford University Press, p. 158.
[9] Ibid, p. 130.
[10] Crawford, Michael. 1978. *The Roman Republic*. Cambridge, MA: Harvard University Press, p. 46.
[11] Ibid, p. 124.
[12] Starr, Chester G. 1971. *The Ancient Romans*. New York, NY: Oxford University Press, pp. 82-85.
[13] Crawford, Michael. 1978. *The Roman Republic*. Cambridge, MA: Harvard University Press, p. 162.
[14] Ibid, p. 176.
[15] Ibid, p. 161.
[16] Starr, Chester G. 1971. *The Ancient Romans*. New York, NY: Oxford University Press, pp. 72-73.
[17] Ibid, pp. 116-118.
[18] Ibid, p. 72.
[19] Ibid, p. 116.
[20] Ibid, pp. 78-79.
[21] Ibid, pp. 118-119.
[22] Ibid, p. 73.
[23] Crawford, Michael. 1978. *The Roman Republic*. Cambridge, MA: Harvard University Press, p. 134.
[24] Ibid, pp. 102-108.
[25] Ibid, p. 141.
[26] Starr, Chester G. 1971. *The Ancient Romans*. New York, NY: Oxford University Press, pp. 120-121.
[27] Ibid, p. 87.
[28] Ibid, pp. 86-88.
[29] Ibid, p. 92.
[30] Ibid, p. 132.
[31] Ibid, p. 124.
[32] Goldsworthy, Adrian. 2009. *How Rome Fell*. New Haven, CT: Yale University Press, p.145.
[33] Ibid, pp.48-49
[34] Starr, Chester G. 1971. *The Ancient Romans*. New York, NY: Oxford University Press, p. 104.
[35] Ibid, pp. 152-155.
[36] Goldsworthy, Adrian. 2009. *How Rome Fell*. New Haven, CT: Yale University Press, p 164.
[37] Ibid, pp. 131-132.

[38] Starr, Chester G. 1971. *The Ancient Romans*. New York, NY: Oxford University Press, pp. 144-145.

[39] Ibid, pp. 179-180.

[40] Grant, Michael. 1999. *The Collapse and Recovery of the Roman Empire*. London and New York, NY: Routledge, p. 46.

[41] Starr, Chester G. 1971. *The Ancient Romans*. New York, NY: Oxford University Press, p. 198.

[42] Ibid, p. 197.

[43] Ibid, p. 199.

[44] Ibid, p. 173.

[45] Ibid, p. 142.

[46] Grant, Michael. 1999. *The Collapse and Recovery of the Roman Empire*. London and New York, NY: Routledge, pp. 35-38.

[47] Goldsworthy, Adrian. 2009. *How Rome Fell*. New Haven, CT: Yale University Press, p.164.

[48] Starr, Chester G. 1971. *The Ancient Romans*. New York, NY: Oxford University Press, pp. 197-198.

[49] Ibid, p. 191.

[50] Grant, Michael. 1999. *The Collapse and Recovery of the Roman Empire*. London and New York, NY: Routledge, pp. 3-13.

[51] Ibid, p. 16.

[52] Starr, Chester G. 1971. *The Ancient Romans*. New York, NY: Oxford University Press, p. 207.

9. The 2007 Great Recession versus the Great Depression

"A nationally planned economy is the only salvation of our present situation and the only hope for the future."

-Donald Richberg,
Member of the Roosevelt Administration

The Great Depression embodied a decade of human misery and economic decline that affected all social classes, from the poor to the rich [1]. It started in 1929 and lasted 11 years. The unemployment rate peaked at 26% [2], and poverty became widespread as shantytowns emerged. The homeless scrounged crates, cans, and auto parts, and constructed shantytowns on vacant lots and under bridges. Shantytowns had no water, electricity, and other utilities [3]. Everyone blamed President Hoover and called these shantytowns – Hoovervilles in his honor. People roamed from state to state, searching for work [4]. Breadlines stretched around street corners while some people committed crimes to receive room and board at the jail [5].

Many economists do not know what started the Great Depression and why it lasted so long because a recession usually lasts one or two years. This chapter notes the similarities and differences between the Great Depression and the 2007 Great Recession. The Great Depression started as a mild recession that gradually worsened. The United States may not leave the 2007 Great Recession as it became the prelude to the Second Great Depression.

The Prosperous 1920s

Before the start of the Great Depression, the United States grew enormously. Family incomes significantly rose while the living standards improved for all Americans. We call the 1920s the Era of Prosperity, one of the most prosperous eras in American history.

During the 1920s, American consumers amassed enough wealth to invest in a revolutionary product that transformed the American landscape – the car. With increasing wealth and the advent of mass-production technology, car prices plummeted, leading to a surge in demand. Registered cars skyrocketed from 9 million to 23 million during the 1920s. This surge in car ownership revolutionized transportation and spurred the growth of ancillary industries. The government constructed roads and bridges and installed signs and traffic lights. At the same time, businesses established gas stations, auto parts stores, repair garages, and car dealerships. The automobile industry significantly influenced the U.S. economy during the 1920s and played a critical role in job creation, wealth generation, and the birth of new industries.

During the 1920s, households invested heavily in homes, commercial real estate, and consumer products. Families wanted to escape the confines and stress of the city, and they began migrating to the suburbs. Mortgage financing was pivotal for this migration because a family could buy a house in the suburbs [7]. Of course, every family wanted all the new electronic devices such as radios, cooking devices, vacuum cleaners, washers, dryers, and other appliances [8]. Finance companies helped families finance these consumer products [9]. Finally, large corporations wanted to show their power and financial position by investing in massive office buildings. For example, they built the famous landmark – the Empire State Building during the 1920s [7].

Everyone economically benefited during the prosperous 1920s. However, not everyone shared the benefits equally. With a strong manufacturing sector, the 1920s saw the rise of skilled laborers who earned higher wages than the unskilled. Towards the end of the 1920s, the wealthiest people in the United States also saw the largest gains in wealth. The wealth of the top 1% of the wealthiest people in the United States rose from 32% to 38%. An overvalued stock market contributed to the high salaries for CEOs. Consequently, the 1920s saw the "highest income inequalities in American history" [10].

The 1920s also witnessed a significant shift in societal norms. The divorce rate in America reached its peak during this decade, with one divorce occurring for every six marriages. This trend, along with the influx of new wealth from the stock market, led to a more liberal and carefree lifestyle. The era was marked by increased socializing and a decline in traditional moral values.

As the economy flourished, American families and corporations accumulated debt without much concern. However, the situation took a drastic turn when incomes and wealth began to decline. The stock market crash wiped out paper wealth, and soon after, real estate prices collapsed as the real estate bubble burst. By the end of the 1920s, developers had oversupplied the number of housing plots in the suburbs, leading to a severe economic downturn.

The 1920s were prosperous, and unfortunately, as Newton's Law of Gravity states, what goes up must eventually come down. The Prosperous 1920s came to an explosive close like a shotgun blast on a still, cold night. The Great Depression began with the stock market crash in 1929.

The 1929 Stock Market Crash

The stock market rose dramatically during the 1920s. Stock prices were rising so fast that people spread rumors about shoeshine boys and waitresses becoming millionaires by investing their meager tips in the stock market [12].

In 1927, the Federal Reserve and President Hoover tried to slow the rapidly rising stock prices by increasing interest rates. They believed the market was overvalued and wanted to prevent a stock market bubble [13, 14].

Some believe the U.S. government and Federal Reserve did not want gold to leave the United States because our country was on the gold standard. A higher interest rate would encourage international investors to keep their money in the U.S. economy and not cash in dollars for gold. However, the Federal Reserve's actions had no impact on the economy.

The stock market experienced a bumpy ride during October and crashed on October 29, 1929, which everyone knows infamously as "Black Tuesday" [15]. On that infamous day, investors traded 16 million shares on the New York Stock Exchange, accumulating losses in the billions. The stock market crash struck the country with a profound sense of shock and disbelief, and many viewed the crash as a devastating blow to a once strong U.S. economy [15].

With the stock market crash in 1929, corporate corruption and excessive greed rose to the surface. In response, the U.S. government took decisive action, passing laws requiring corporations to disclose more information to stockholders, and President Roosevelt established the Securities Exchange Commission to police the stock markets. The federal government also passed new laws making insider trading and bear raids illegal, demonstrating a commitment to restoring trust in the market [16].

Many similarities exist between the Stock Market Crash 1929 and the stock market decline in October 2008. Technically, the stock market did not crash in 2008, but stock prices declined in value significantly. The Dow Jones peaked roughly at 14,000 and bottomed out around 7,000, declining by 50% in value, and this severe drop reverberates throughout the economy. Declining stock prices have two impacts on the U.S. economy:

- ➢ **Impact 1:** People and businesses holding stock see their paper wealth dissipate in the air like smoke. As their paper wealth disappears, people and businesses reduce their consumption, especially luxury goods. It is no coincidence that the travel industry, durable goods like cars, and business investment have taken massive hits since the 2007 Great Recession.

- ➢ **Impact 2:** Working people invest their pension plans into the financial markets. With massive losses in the financial markets, many people nearing retirement had to delay their retirement plans, a situation that evokes sympathy. Furthermore, people keep their money out of the stock market and hide it under their mattresses.

The Banking System

At the onset of the Great Depression, the government took a proactive stance by postponing the liquidation of bad business loans.

It also encouraged financial institutions to continue lending to businesses, even those that were not good for investment. This strategy aimed to maintain high investment spending, which was expected to stimulate the stock market's recovery.

The Federal Reserve stood on the sidelines, allowing many banks to fail during the Great Depression. However, most people do not realize the United States was on the gold standard. The Fed could not increase the money supply or provide emergency loans to banks because it did not have enough gold. The government fixed the exchange rate between gold and U.S. dollars at 1 ounce = $20. Furthermore, people lost faith in the banking system and transferred their money into gold. People withdrew gold from the Federal Reserve and hoarded it. In 1933, President Roosevelt declared the holding or hoarding of gold illegal, and the United States left the gold standard.

Unlike the Great Depression, the United States is no longer constrained by the gold standard. This means that the Federal Reserve now has the freedom to issue money and grant loans as it deems necessary. And it's not holding back.

Interest rates drop to historic low levels during severe economic contractions. The Federal Reserve discount rate fell from 4.5% to 1.5% during the Great Depression [18]. The discount rate is the interest rate the Federal Reserve charges financial institutions for emergency loans. Similarly, the Federal Reserve discount rate nosedived during the 2007 Great Recession as the discount rate dropped to 0.5% in December 2008 [19].

Usually, interest rates move together. As the discount rate falls, other interest rates fall. This is excellent news for borrowers because their loan payments become cheaper. However, this represents bad news for lenders, investors, and savers because they earn less interest income, shrinking their profits and incomes. Nevertheless, the problem with low interest rates signals two worrisome issues for the 2007 Great Recession, which includes the following:

> **Problem 1:** The Federal Reserve System has injected trillions of dollars into the banking system even though the U.S. economy still sheds jobs. Foreclosures and

bankruptcies continue climbing. Moreover, the Federal Reserve granted over $2 trillion in emergency loans to financial institutions and did not disclose which banks had received loans, believing depositors and investors would panic if they discovered their banks were in financial trouble.

> **Problem 2:** Lower interest rates may not spur economic development for two factors. First, Americans have borrowed the maximum they can borrow. Experiencing troubles repaying their debt, they will not add to it. Second, house and car prices are falling. It would be foolish for consumers to get loans on assets that are losing value. Borrowers would wait until the prices hit rock bottom before taking on new loans. Furthermore, banks may not lend for assets with falling prices, just in case they must foreclose on these assets.

Deflation

During the Great Depression, the U.S. experienced a sharp deflation [20]. Deflation occurs as prices drop, and economists consider it a two-edged sword. On one hand, falling prices benefit consumers because consumers purchase more products as they become cheaper. On the other hand, deflation harms an economy because lower prices squeeze business profits. A business cannot survive if it cannot profit, so it must reduce its costs. A company has three methods to lower its costs.

> **Method 1:** A business could adopt new technology that increases efficiency so it can produce more using the same resources. Usually, businesses do not invest during economic downturns. Business managers are uncertain about future profits and would rather save money than invest in new technology.

> **Method 2:** Labor is a business's largest cost, so companies reduce wage rates or lay off workers. If employers lay off

workers, workers earn less to buy goods and services, which contracts the economy. Rising unemployment causes another alarming trend for the U.S. consumer economy.

> **Method 3:** Businesses relocate to countries with cheaper operating costs. In our case, that would be China. Unfortunately, the business creates jobs and wealth in China and not within the United States, which further damages the U.S. manufacturing economy.

During the Great Depression, severe deflation led to massive layoffs and a significant drop in production. Production of durable goods fell by 50%, nondurable goods fell by 20%, and retail sales dropped by 25% [21].

During the Great Depression, the U.S. government attempted to alleviate the situation by passing the Smoot-Hawley Act. This legislation was intended to bolster domestic industries by imposing tariffs to protect U.S. agriculture and manufacturing from international competition. However, the unintended consequence was reduced global trade, leading to further unemployment and income losses [21].

Businesses and farmers earn greater profits by selling commodities for higher prices. Businesses use some of these profits to pay the stockholders of corporations, which helps boost the stock market. Furthermore, businesses use some of the profits to pay higher wages to the workers. Moreover, farmers earning greater incomes would slow down many farmer bankruptcies and farm foreclosures. However, the tariffs backfired. Trading partners with the United States also passed similar tariffs, causing international trade to collapse. We do not know how many farmers and domestic businesses benefited from the tariffs, but the loss of the export industry led to further unemployment and income losses.

The United States is experiencing a mild deflation, and businesses are not absorbing the lower prices by adopting new technology. Moreover, retailers reported disappointing sales for the 2008 Christmas, and Chrysler and GM filed for bankruptcy in 2009. Moreover, many companies left the United States and opened new factories in foreign countries like China. Then they began exporting cheap Chinese products to the United States. With companies leaving the United States, companies create fewer jobs and lower incomes for Americans. Incidentally, the tax base contracts as people pay fewer taxes to the government. It is no coincidence that many states and local governments are going broke in the United States.

While the U.S. government did not implement widespread trade restrictions during the 2007 Great Recession, the situation could change. The 2012 presidential debates saw expressions of discontent with China over the loss of U.S. manufacturing jobs, hinting at a potential shift in trade policy.

Farmers

The Great Depression, a devastating period, particularly for U.S. farmers. Even before the stock market crash, they were grappling with declining agricultural prices. As prices plummeted and a severe drought ravaged the Midwest, bankruptcies and foreclosures forced many farmers off their lands. Yet, in the face of such adversity, some farmers showed remarkable resilience, arming themselves and becoming militant, while others sought new opportunities in states like California [23].

The U.S. government responded to falling agricultural prices by interfering with the agricultural markets. The government uses two techniques to boost farmers' incomes. First, the government expands farm exports by supplying international consumers. More consumers mean higher prices. Unfortunately, during the Great Depression, the U.S. government destroyed free trade. Second, the government boosted farmers' incomes by increasing the prices of agricultural products, subsidizing cheap credit to farmers, or subsidizing farm cooperatives [24]. A cooperative is an organization that unifies the farmers into one supplier, and one supplier becomes a monopoly that raises the selling price. The government usually considers monopolies wrong, except the ones it supports.

During the Great Depression, President Hoover let the U.S. government intervene heavily in the butter, cotton, grape, wheat, and wool markets, but the market price of these commodities continued falling [25].

President Roosevelt took government control one step further when he came into power. The government set production quotas on corn, cotton, dairy products, hogs, rice, tobacco, and wheat. The federal government paid subsidies to farmers to stop farmers from planting crops on their land. If farmers produced too much, the government would buy the excess and destroy it. Government intervention aggressively boosted farm incomes, but consumers paid greater food prices. Unfortunately, as some people were starving, the U.S. government destroyed food.

The U.S. government still imposes price controls, and they remain ineffective because agricultural prices have been dropping since the 1990s. Most economists consider price controls useless because an artificially high price causes farmers to supply more. As the supply rises, the market price falls. Then the government enters a ridiculous situation when it stockpiles massive agricultural products or destroys them to bring the supply back down.

Since the 2007 Great Recession, the echoes of the Great Depression continue to reverberate. Many agricultural prices are plummeting, and some farmers are still awaiting payment for commodities they shipped to the markets in 2008. The repercussions of the Great Recession are still being felt, with some companies having succumbed to bankruptcy.

Employment

During the Great Depression, more and more people became unemployed over time, and the unemployment rate peaked at 26% in 1932. With scarce jobs and applicants lining up for one job, the power balance between the employer and employee shifted towards the employer. Employers reduced wages, boosted workloads, increased work hours, and reduced benefits. Employees become powerless as numerous applicants line up for their jobs [26].

One particular company turned its employees into slaves. During the Great Depression, people living near the coalfields in Harlan, Kentucky, had a harsh place to live. Coal-mining companies owned the miners' homes and local grocery stores. Companies extracted every penny from the miners by lowering their wages, forcing them to live in the companies' homes, and selling them groceries at the companies' stores [27]. Companies completely controlled the economic affairs of their employees.

Teenagers and children did not find jobs and stopped attending school during the Great Depression. State budget problems caused many schools to close their doors. Furthermore, teenagers and children accepted the hobo lifestyle and drifted back and forth across the United States [28].

African Americans experienced more discrimination during the Great Depression as jobs became scarce. They paid more money in rent compared to white families as they rented rat-infested basements and used cans as toilets. Many African-American families rented or shared their apartment space with other families to help pay for rent. They also turned to charities and other public relief programs [29].

President Hoover in 1929 encouraged businesses not to lay people off or reduce wages. High wages maintain strong consumer spending [17]. If businesses still employ people, the people retain their purchasing power. If employers lay off workers or cut their wages and hours, they cannot buy houses, cars, appliances, and other goods. The U.S. government granted concessions and subsidies to businesses [17]. President Roosevelt took this a step further and tried to boost the number of jobs by creating public works jobs, imposing regulations on businesses, lowering the workweek to 40 hours, and passing child labor laws. Finally, the U.S. government cut the immigration quota by 90% in 1930 because they believed cheap foreign labor reduced wages [30].

President Obama has not influenced businesses in terms of employment. Many corporations continue laying off thousands of employees. Massive layoffs negatively impact an economy. For instance, laid-off workers will reduce their purchases of houses, cars, appliances, travel, and other luxury goods. As revenues to these industries fall, their profits decrease, causing these industries to reduce their workforce. Then more laid-off workers reduce their spending further. Unfortunately, this vicious cycle continues indefinitely.

If workers remain employed, they see these job losses and fear losing their jobs. Consequently, they reduce their spending and increase their savings, adding more misery to a weak U.S. consumer economy. A consumer economy cannot grow if people save as much money as possible. Maynard Keynes called this the Paradox of Thrift.

As a country economically declines and stagnates, citizens pick on an ethnic group and blame them for a country's financial problems and malaise. Nevertheless, the United States represents a giant melting pot of cultures and peoples, and the government and the people cannot blame a particular ethnic group. Instead, they blame the illegal immigrants. For example, the State of Arizona passed a new strict immigration law that allows officers to ask for a person's citizenship status and makes it illegal to help or transport undocumented residents. The state will incarcerate more priests and nuns when they help feed and clothe people in need, like illegal immigrants. God does not care about a person's immigration status.

Rumors abound that illegal immigrants are fleeing Arizona because of the new strict state laws. The people and government of Arizona do not understand that the state will lose workers and customers. Business costs will rise as they hire more expensive, legal labor and fewer immigrants will buy and rent homes, shop at stores, and buy cars. Consequently, the economy of Arizona could tank further as a portion of its population flees.

Many states have cracked down on residents applying for or renewing their driver's licenses, which our state leaders say is reducing the number of illegal residents. The state wants numerous documents, such as a recently certified birth certificate, marriage and divorce papers, licenses, documents showing proof of residency, etc. Most people do not realize we have adopted the Soviet system of bureaucracy. One trip to a Soviet bureaucracy resulted in multiple trips to other bureaucracies. Then citizens must plead or argue with the bureaucrats for the numerous certified documents.

What is interesting is illegal immigration has always been a problem since the 1980s. No one cared about immigration until the 2007 Great Recession struck the economy. People have become upset over illegal immigration, which is becoming a nationally charged issue.

The labor market remained horrible in 2012. Although the U.S. unemployment rate was 8.3%, roughly 12 million workers left the labor market. Many college graduates did not find jobs, while foreign workers fled the United States, returning to their home countries. Four years after the start of the 2007 Great Recession, the jobs have not returned, and they are not likely to return.

Rising Taxes

At the start of the Great Depression, President Hoover passed minor tax cuts. The personal income tax rate fell from 5% to 4%, while the corporate income tax rate fell from 12% to 11%. The theory behind the tax cuts is that people and businesses will have more money. When consumers have more money, they spend more, creating higher demand for goods and services. If businesses have more money, they hire more workers and invest in machines and equipment. Investment allows firms to operate more efficiently and produce additional goods and services. Consequently, tax cuts should boost a weak economy. At the beginning of the Great Depression, the U.S. federal government still had a surplus that became smaller after the tax cuts [31].

As the Great Depression persisted, the federal government found itself grappling with budget deficits. The severe downturn in manufacturing and the staggering number of bankruptcies had eroded the tax base. In a dramatic reversal in 1931, President Hoover implemented the largest peacetime tax increase in American history. This included new taxes on gas, tires, malt, stock transfers, bank checks, and real estate, as well as a hike in income tax rates. Hoover's aim was to stimulate consumption and discourage savings, leading to the imposition of taxes on investment [17].

President Roosevelt passed a slew of new taxes when he came into office. Roosevelt did not want high government debt, so he created numerous government agencies and large, expensive public works projects. Thus, Roosevelt increased income and estate taxes and imposed an excise tax on almost everything. Some of the excise taxes were on lubricating oil, malt syrup, brewer's wort, tires, toilet articles, furs, jewelry, automobiles, trucks, radio and phonograph equipment, refrigerators, sporting goods, cameras, firearms, matches, candy, chewing gum, soft drinks, and electricity [33].

When a government imposes numerous excise taxes, it creates a complex tax system. Each tax comes with its own set of rules and tax schedules that businesses must navigate. A simpler alternative could be a universal sales tax that applies to all transactions, reducing the administrative burden on businesses.

Tax hikes are disruptive to economies during recessions. If households and businesses are hurting financially, hiking taxes intensifies the hurt. Unfortunately, the 2007 Great Recession is lowering incomes while foreclosures and bankruptcies continue soaring, and several industries teeter on collapse. Many states and local governments are hurting financially. Consequently, many state politicians dreamed up new taxes or expanded old ones and hiked fees and fines. Although the federal government reduced taxes, states nullified the tax decrease with hikes in state and local taxes.

President Obama passed a national healthcare plan that expands coverage to everyone, including 35 million without health insurance. The government will charge businesses additional taxes and fees to pay for this plan and expand Medicare and Medicaid bureaucracies. These policies work against the economy and hinder economic growth.

President Obama's decision to raise taxes in the midst of a struggling economy is a significant move. Since the 2008 Financial Crisis, the U.S. federal government has been operating with trillion-dollar deficits. This has raised concerns among investors about the financial health of the U.S. government, potentially leading them to stop buying U.S. government securities. In such a scenario, the federal government would be left with three options: Increasing taxes, reducing budget expenditures, or compelling the central bank, the Federal Reserve, to buy U.S. securities, which could result in high inflation.

Growing Government

President Hoover used the federal government's power to shorten the Great Depression. Hoover asked states to expand state public works programs [34] that created jobs for unemployed workers by building new bridges, roads, and parks. Moreover, the Hoover Dam was constructed [5]. Workers who have more money buy more products, creating a demand for more goods and services. In addition, the state has more roads, sidewalks, and infrastructure.

Franklin Roosevelt easily won the presidency because many people blamed the Great Depression on capitalism and excessive greed. He took Hoover's plan and greatly expanded it. President Roosevelt created numerous government agencies and a slew of new taxes to pay for them. Only the prominent government agencies are listed below because the list is quite long:

> **The Federal National Mortgage Association** (i.e., Fannie Mae) is an agency that grants mortgages to the poor. Many banks collapsed or stopped lending during the Great Depression, and Fannie Mae tried to get the housing market growing again by granting mortgages.

> **The Federal Deposits Insurance Corporation** (FDIC) insures banks' deposits. Deposit insurance helps prevent bank runs. A bank run occurs when all the depositors show up at their bank simultaneously to withdraw their deposits because they believe the bank will fail. A bank lends most of its money out and cannot pay all the depositors when they show up simultaneously. Thus, a bank run always causes a bank failure. Depositors believe their deposits are safe because FDIC insures them. If the bank fails, then FDIC pays the depositors their money.

> **The Federal Bureau of Investigation** (FBI) tracks down criminals who violate federal laws. The FBI evolved from previous enforcement agencies. During the Great Depression, many people lost their money when their banks failed. Thus, bank robbers like John Dillinger, Babyface

Nelson, and Bonnie and Clyde became folk heroes because they struck back at the banks. The federal government, through FDIC-insured bank deposits, made bank robbing a federal crime. President Roosevelt wanted the FBI to track down and capture those bank robbers.

> **Securities and Exchange Commission** (SEC) polices the stock markets. SEC agents investigate financial fraud and manipulation of stock prices.
> **Federal Communications Commission** (FCC) regulates radio and TV transmissions.
> **The National Recovery Agency** (NRA) was a government agency that set prices and wages for businesses and labor and imposed numerous regulations and production standards for all goods and services. This agency no longer exists because the U.S. Supreme Court ruled it unconstitutional in 1936.
> **The Public Works Administration** (PWA) was a government agency that contracted with private companies to build 34,599 large public works projects. The government dissolved the PWA during World War II because the war pulled the U.S. economy out of the Depression, and the government no longer needed these jobs.
> **The National Labor Relations Board** was a government board that expanded labor unions. Labor unions boost workers' wages and benefits through strikes, which are a coercive technique to force businesses to join unions. If a business does not agree with the labor union, the workers shut down production and walk off the job site, financially harming the employer because it has no products to sell.

The U.S. economy became more socialized during the Great Depression, and it improved slightly. However, the government did not pull the economy out of the Depression. World War II brought the country out of the Great Depression. As Hitler began annexing Austria, Sudetenland, and Poland, the European war machines fired up, and Europe started buying U.S. military goods. Then U.S. manufacturing was infused with money and jobs.

After the 2007 Great Recession, President Obama founded a new agency, the Bureau of Consumer Financial Protection, to protect consumers from banks and finance companies. Many banks and finance companies that experienced the 2008 Financial Crisis were the same ones that charged excessively high fees and were involved in loan fraud. The government should allow these financial institutions to go bankrupt. Bankruptcy gets rid of bad businesses and institutions, making room for good businesses to thrive and grow.

President Obama passed his healthcare plan requiring all Americans in the United States to purchase health insurance after 2014. However, some experts believe the healthcare plan has created massive business uncertainty. No one wants to hire new workers because businessmen and managers do not know how their costs will change once the government implements the healthcare plan. Consequently, the labor market in 2012 was the worst this author has seen in his life.

Many people think capitalism failed and the government, like Superman, would swoop down and fix all our problems. Although the federal and state governments are not likely to establish new bureaucracies, we have enough bureaucracies to create a government-controlled economy. We expect President Obama to expand the powers of the federal bureaucracies continually while the state governments continue expanding theirs.

Conclusion

Many experts and economists predicted a turnaround in the U.S. economy in 2010, but it has not materialized. Many companies continually leave the United States, then lay off workers, and most states operate budget deficits. Similar to the Great Depression, many experts predicted an improving economy. However, as the economy improved slightly, something else collapsed. People needed a decade to realize something severe struck the economy.

Economists do not know what started the Great Depression or why it lasted so long. Every story has two sides, and in many cases, nobody knows which story is the correct one. For example, many people view President Roosevelt as a leader who helped ease the Great Depression. He used the federal government to stop prices and wages from dropping, created public works jobs, and established various new alphabet-soup government agencies.

President Roosevelt delivered a message of hope to the citizens, but some economists believe his reforms extended the Great Depression. The U.S. economy entered a recession in 1937 when it was still in the Great Depression. If the United States were in a depression, how could it enter a recession? These economists believe the Great Depression should have lasted several years if the government had not interfered with the economy.

Some great minds, like Irving Fisher, believed depressions have two characteristics that wreak havoc on an economy:

> **Deflation** – an economy experiences falling prices. Deflation hurts business profits because their revenues drop from decreasing prices. Then businesses lay off workers. More unemployed workers have less income to buy products, and businesses experience a further decrease in sales. Then this vicious cycle continues.

> **Credit-Debt Cycle** – too much credit allows asset bubbles to form, until an economy reaches a saturation point when they cannot borrow anymore. Then the asset bubble pops.

Credit-debt cycles are vicious to an economy because an expansion of credit allows industries to expand rapidly. For example, during the 1920s, consumers borrowed, so they purchased homes, appliances, and cars. Factories quickly expanded production from the greater demand for their products. This expansion created manufacturing jobs and wealth. However, consumers have reached a point where they cannot borrow anymore. Then demand for these products plummeted, sparking widespread unemployment and bankruptcies. It sounds suspiciously similar to the situation in 2008 when American consumers had accumulated too much debt and stopped buying in the consumer economy.

The credit-debt cycle occurred during the Stock Market Crash in 1929. Investors borrowed funds to invest in the stock market by borrowing on the margin. For example, an investor invested $1,000 into stocks using $100 of his own money and borrowing $900 on the margin. Of course, borrowing on the margin allows people to overextend themselves, but everybody wins as the stock prices continue soaring. As stock prices keep climbing, more and more people invest more money into the market. Eventually, the money stops flowing into the market. As stock prices start falling, investors panic and withdraw all their money from the market, crashing the stock price. Then many financial companies go bankrupt as investors cannot repay their margins.

A credit-debt cycle occurred during the U.S. housing boom between 2001 and 2007 as banks created new exotic securities to attract investors to the mortgage market. Unfortunately, asset bubbles can occur for any commodity. The first recorded asset bubble was the Tulip Mania in the 17th-century Netherlands. An asset bubble occurred from flower bulbs [35]!

References

[1] Nishi 2001, Dennis. 2001. *The Great Depression*. Greenhaven Press, Inc: San Diego, p. 27.

[2] Rothbard 1972, Murray. 1972. *America's Great Depression*. Sheed and Ward, Inc: Kansas City, p. 1.

[3] Nishi 2001, Dennis. 2001. *The Great Depression*. Greenhaven Press, Inc: San Diego, p. 17.

[4] Ibid, p. 18.

[5] Ibid, p. 15.

[6] Hall , Thomas E. and J. David Ferguson. 2002. *The 1920s: A New Era of Prosperity*. The Crash of 1929. Greenhaven Press, Inc: San Diego, pp. 22-24.

[7] Ibid, pp. 24-25.

[8] Ibid, pp. 22-25.

[9] Gerdes, Louise I. 2002. *The Crash of 1929*. Greenhaven Press, Inc: San Diego, pp. 12-13.

[10] Hall , Thomas E. and J. David Ferguson. 2002. *The 1920s: A New Era of Prosperity*. The Crash of 1929. Greenhaven Press, Inc: San Diego, pp. 26-27.

[11] Klingaman 2002, William K. 2002. "Everybody Ought to be Rich:" *The Midsummer Boom. The Crash of 1929*. Greenhaven Press, Inc: San Diego, pp. 38-39.

[12] Nishi 2001, Dennis. 2001. *The Great Depression*. Greenhaven Press, Inc: San Diego, p. 31.

[13] Rothbard 1972, Murray. 1972. *America's Great Depression*. Sheed and Ward, Inc: Kansas City, p. 145.

[14] Nishi 2001, Dennis. 2001. *The Great Depression*. Greenhaven Press, Inc: San Diego, p. 12.

[15] Gerdes, Louise I. 2002. *The Crash of 1929*. Greenhaven Press, Inc: San Diego, p. 11.

[16] Axon, Gordon V. 2002. *Establishing Government Regulations and Safeguards. The Crash of 1929*. Greenhaven Press, Inc: San Diego, pp.129-133.

[17] Rothbard 1972, Murray. 1972. *America's Great Depression*. Sheed and Ward, Inc: Kansas City, pp. 26-27.

[18] Ibid, pp.212-213.

[19] Board of Governors. December 18, 2008. "Press Release." Federal Reserve System. Available at http://www.federalreserve.gov/newsevents/press/monetary/20081218a.htm (access date 01/09/09).

[20] Rothbard 1972, Murray. 1972. *America's Great Depression*. Sheed and Ward, Inc: Kansas City, p. 231.

[21] Ibid, pp. 230-237.

[22] Ibid, pp. 213-214.

[23] Nishi 2001, Dennis. 2001. *The Great Depression*. Greenhaven Press, Inc: San Diego, pp. 120-121.

[24] Rothbard 1972, Murray. 1972. *America's Great Depression*. Sheed and Ward, Inc: Kansas City, p. 196.

[25] Ibid, pp.204-207.

[26] Nishi 2001, Dennis. 2001. *The Great Depression*. Greenhaven Press, Inc: San Diego, p. 87.

[27] Gates, Sudy. 2001. *A Hard Life in the Harlan Mines. The Great Depression*. Greenhaven Press, Inc: San Diego, pp. 144-118.

[28] Nishi 2001, Dennis. 2001. *The Great Depression*. Greenhaven Press, Inc: San Diego, p. 158.

[29] Hedgeman 2001, Anna Arnold. 2001. *Hard Times in Harlem. The Great Depression*. Greenhaven Press, Inc: San Diego, pp. 82-85.

[30] Rothbard 1972, Murray. 1972. *America's Great Depression*. Sheed and Ward, Inc: Kansas City, pp. 215-216.

[31] Ibid, p. 225.

[32] Ibid, p. 231.

[33] Tax History Museum. "1901-1932: The Income Tax Arrives." Available at http://www.taxanalysts.com/museum/1901-1932.htm (access date 12/31/08).

[34] Rothbard 1972, Murray. 1972. *America's Great Depression.* Sheed and
Ward, Inc: Kansas City, p. 193.
[35] Wikipedia. 2008. "Tulip Mania." Available at www.wikipedia.org (access
date 12/26/08).

"A business that makes nothing but money is a poor business."
-Henry Ford

The 2008 Financial Crisis developed into the perfect storm because five unrelated factors created a massive housing bubble in the United States. The five factors include the following:

➢ **Factor 1:** Banks were so eager to lend money for a mortgage that they seemed to have abandoned all caution. If the applicant had a pulse and a paycheck stub, they were granted a mortgage. In the past, banks meticulously scrutinized all applicants, demanding tax returns, stable employment, and even the number of times an applicant had been married.

➢ **Factor 2:** Wall Street Bankers created new exotic financial securities they marketed. As incomes and wealth rose in Europe, the Middle East, and Asia, investors bought trillions of these exotic securities. Wall Street bankers channeled this money into the housing market, rapidly appreciating the housing values.

➢ **Factor 3:** Despite their lack of understanding of the exotic securities, investors poured their money into them because the rating agencies had given them a triple-A rating. These securities were always packaged to have a triple-A credit rating, but their complexity meant that few people truly comprehended them.

➢ **Factor 4:** The U.S. government, in a surprising move, did not regulate the financial markets for the new exotic securities. U.S. regulatory agencies stood on the sidelines and watched these markets mushroom into trillions of dollars, a decision that would have far-reaching consequences.

> **Factor 5:** Statistician David Li invented a method to price these exotic securities using advanced mathematics. He replied that Wall Street banks were not using his method correctly. His method prices securities using historical values. Consequently, the prices of securities rely on increasing property values because property values have continuously risen since the Great Depression.

The United States entered the 2007 Great Recession. As the unemployment rate soared while incomes fell, some people stopped paying their mortgages, which shocked the financial markets. Foreign investors began questioning what they bought, stopping money flow into Wall Street and precipitating the 2008 Financial Crisis.

The U.S. government used the 2008 Financial Crisis to take over the U.S. economy. Politicians and regulators told the public that the free market had failed and that the government must step in to fix it. Rampant, excessive greed on Wall Street put the whole country in jeopardy.

The U.S. government will not tell us they knew about this problem because a smaller event happened in 1998. Hedge fund, Long-Term Capital Management, crashed and burned during the 1998 Asian Financial Crisis. The hedge fund invested $1.25 trillion in various exotic financial securities. New York Federal Reserve organized a $3.6 billion bailout that stopped the economic disaster from spreading to the U.S. banks.

One person in the United States government saw the problems and flaws with these exotic securities and pushed for new regulations. Congress, the Department of Treasury, and the Federal Reserve immediately stopped her. Political leaders who stopped the new rules are the same ones who criticized Wall Street in 2008. Frontline produced an excellent documentary, *The Forewarning in 1998: Long-Term Financial Capital*, which covers this event. Suppose government leaders had listened and adopted laws to regulate these exotic securities. The 2007 Great Recession may not have been as severe in that case.

Pushing for Homeownership

The U.S. government planted the seeds that sprouted into the 2008 Financial Crisis. These seeds came from the American Dream, where all American families should own their own homes. Thus, politicians and government officials help perpetuate this dream by passing favorable laws for homeownership.

The Community Reinvestment Act (CRA) of 1977 forced banks to lend to low-income households [1]. On the surface, the government created an excellent law because banks should grant mortgages to low-income families. Furthermore, cities are teeming with poor neighborhoods and poor households; thus, this law could help banks invest in blighted neighborhoods and help transform them into thriving communities. This law makes this investment possible without using taxpayer money.

Some community organizations, like the Association of Community Organizations for Reform Now (ACORN), used the Community Reinvestment Act to strong-arm banks into granting loans to low-income households. If a bank wants to merge with another or open a new bank branch, the U.S. government can approve this activity. However, if a community organization believed this bank did not grant enough loans to poor people, it would petition the U.S. government, claiming it violated the Community Reinvestment Act. Thus, an organization could delay bank mergers and bank branch expansions indefinitely with these petitions [1].

Banks are caught in a catch-22. Low-income households are more likely to default on loans than the middle-class and wealthy, but not making enough loans to poor people could jeopardize future business expansions. Moreover, banks could not charge higher interest rates to compensate for this higher default risk. Some low-income households are minorities, and the public and government leaders would call the banks racists for charging higher interest rates.

The Community Reinvestment Act also strong-armed two public corporations: the Federal National Mortgage Association (Fannie Mae) and the Federal Home Loan Mortgage Corporation

(Freddie Mac). President Clinton used the law during the 1990s to pressure Fannie Mae and Freddie Mac to expand loans to low-income households, predominantly black and Hispanic households. Consequently, Fannie Mae and Freddie Mac expanded mortgages until low-income households comprised at least 42% of their loans [2, 3].

Fannie Mae and Freddie Mac provide mortgages to low-income households, making the mortgage market more liquid. Investors prefer liquid assets because they can sell quickly with little transaction costs.

Mortgages were traditionally illiquid assets because once a bank grants a mortgage, it is stuck with the mortgage until the bank forecloses on the home or the homeowner repays it. Investors avoided buying mortgages because they are long-term loans and entail high risk. If a homeowner stops paying his mortgage, investors can incur large losses. Several bad loans in a portfolio can bankrupt a mortgage fund.

An ingenious innovation came along that allowed banks to grant mortgages to anyone. Moreover, this innovation allowed the banks to earn enormous, short-term profits and involved little risk. Consequently, banks quickly approved mortgages for low-income households. Banks removed their stringent loan guidelines, such as verifying borrowers' income, ignoring employment history, and not requiring borrowers to put any money down.

Banks granted 100% financing for homes to anyone. Families that a bank would never approve for a mortgage before the 1990s could get a mortgage, although they were more likely to default. This class of loans evolved into the subprime loan market. As home foreclosures soared during 2008, everyone dubbed these subprime loans toxic mortgages.

Mortgage Asset-Backed Securities

Banks create new security when they package loans with a known cash flow into a fund. Cash flow originates from the borrowers repaying their debts. Consequently, once a bank grants a new mortgage, it places it into a fund to get rid of it. Then investors buy into the fund by purchasing the fund's securities. If the fund is a total of mortgages, then banks call this a mortgage asset-backed security.

A fund issues different types of securities called tranches. A tranche is a French term meaning a portion or slice. Each tranche has a security associated with a risk level, and thus, each tranche of securities has a different credit rating. Some securities are rated AAA and pay the lowest return to investors. However, investors are first in line if the fund goes bust. The fund also issues risky securities that pay a higher return, but investors can lose their investment if the fund goes bankrupt. A good question is – how can the same fund issue AAA and junk-rated securities if it holds the same assets in the fund?

Mortgage asset-backed securities caused banks to expand their mortgage lending. When the borrowers pay their mortgages, the payment goes into the fund, and the fund managers pay a return to the investors. The bank gets its money back from the mortgages and can use it to grant new mortgages. As long as most borrowers pay their mortgages, these funds remain solvent as investors earn an investment return.

Banks earn profits from the closing-cost fees from a new mortgage and fund management expenses. Of course, the banks do not earn profits from the cash flow of a mortgage; the fund investors do. For example, if a family bought a $100,000 home with a 7% interest rate and a 30-year mortgage, their monthly payment equals $665. This does not include property taxes, homeowner's insurance, and other fees. However, the homeowner pays a total of $139,509 of interest to the investors' fund over the life of the loan.

Banks offer homeowners the adjustable-rate mortgages (ARMs) that start with low interest rates, called teaser rates. An ARM mortgage payment starts with a low interest rate, resulting in low monthly payments. Then several years later, the mortgage interest rate resets to a higher level, raising the monthly payments. For example, the monthly payment for a $300,000 mortgage for 30 years with an interest rate of 3% is $1,265. If the interest rate climbs to 6% two years later, the homeowner's monthly payment rises to $1,722 monthly. Once the ARM sets higher, families are struck hard financially. Banks and real estate agents persuaded homeowners to accept ARMs because they could refinance into fixed-rate loans several years later. Unfortunately, the mortgage market collapsed in 2008, and refinancing became unavailable.

The biggest players in mortgage asset-backed securities included the private banks Countrywide Financial, Lehman Brothers, and Wells Fargo and the public corporations Fannie Mae and Freddie Mac. When the United States entered the 2007 Great Recession, they suffered billion-dollar losses.

Nothing is wrong with asset-backed securities. The problem was that the banks, Fannie Mae and Freddie Mac, extended too much credit to poor people. Poor people are vulnerable to downturns in an economy because recessions boost layoffs while jobs become scarce. Subsequently, people have trouble repaying their debt. Furthermore, homeowners cannot pay their mortgages if they lose their jobs and cannot find a new one. Consequently, bankruptcies and foreclosures rise, putting severe financial strain on mortgage companies.

The 2007 Great Recession met severe punishment for Fannie Mae and Freddie Mac. Both held approximately $6 trillion in mortgages as loan default rates soared from 5% to 20% in 2009. Consequently, both Fannie and Freddie hemorrhaged massive losses daily. David Kellermann, former Chief Financial Officer of Freddie Mac, committed suicide in April 2009 [4]. As of January 2010, the losses of both Fannie and Freddie exceeded $400 billion [5], which equaled $1,333 for every man, woman, and child in the United States.

The U.S. federal government nationalized both agencies in September 2008 by annexing them to the federal government. U.S. Treasury Secretary became the CEO of these two companies, eliminated the dividends, and bought $100 million of preferred stock in both companies [6]. Preferred stock elevates investors higher up on the liquidation ladder. Hence, the government has better investment protection if a bankruptcy court liquidates the company.

Collateralized Debt Obligations (CDOs)

The story becomes a little crazier. Investment banks wanted to profit from the U.S. housing market. An investment bank differs from a traditional commercial bank in that it helps corporations issue new stocks or bonds and helps city, county, and state governments issue new bonds. It is a marketing agent for new financial securities. On the other hand, a commercial bank accepts deposits and makes loans.

The U.S. government split the functions of investment and commercial banking during the Great Depression by passing the Glass-Steagall Act of 1933. The federal government believed banks assumed too much risk, which led to massive bank failures during the Great Depression. For instance, if a bank helped a company issue new bonds, it would push them onto its customers. Unfortunately, the federal government repealed the Glass-Steagall Act at the end of the 1990s, allowing investment banks to expand into new activities, including commercial banking. Despite the law, insider trading, conflicts of interest, and excessive greed have perpetually plagued investment bankers on Wall Street since the Great Depression.

Investment banks created a new exotic security, Collateralized Debt Obligations (CDOs). They purchased mortgage asset-backed securities from commercial banks and added other forms of debt. Then they pooled the assets into a fund and sold them to investors. Investment bankers created a new asset-backed security from old asset-backed securities.

Investment banks earned huge profits from the origination and management fees of CDOs. Furthermore, CDOs were low-risk to the investment banks because the investors who purchased the securities assumed all the risk. Investment banks got their money back and used it to set up another CDO fund. The main players of CDOs were Bank of America, Bear Stearns, Citigroup, Deutsche Bank, Lehman Brothers, Merrill Lynch, and Wachovia [7].

A CDO fund issues different tranches, each reflecting a different security with a risk level and credit rating. Furthermore, the investment bankers marketed the CDOs outside the United States to avoid U.S. taxes and regulations.

The U.S. government assesses taxes on foreign companies if they are involved in a trade or business with the United States. However, if a foreign company invests in stocks and bonds, it does not pay U.S. taxes because the U.S. government does not consider financial securities a trade or business. This loophole may exist because the U.S. government wants international investors to buy U.S. Treasury bonds. The U.S. government heavily sells U.S. government securities to foreigners.

Investment bankers always packaged CDOs with an AAA rating [8], attracting international investors. Some experts believe the rating agencies, Standard & Poor and Moody's, participated in fraud, were inept, or had trouble accurately assessing the actual risk of CDOs. Hence, investment bankers always blended subprime mortgages with high-quality mortgage pools to obtain the AAA grade.

Investment banks went into overdrive. The CDO market quickly mushroomed from $552 billion to $2 trillion in 2006 as foreign investors poured money into the CDO funds. Consequently, CDOs fed much money into the U.S. housing market, raising housing values.

Investment and commercial banks needed to grant more mortgages to keep this system going. They kept lowering their lending standards and granted anyone a loan. The joke among Houston's realtors was if a homebuyer had a heartbeat and a paycheck stub in their pocket, then they had a mortgage loan. Furthermore, many homeowners cashed out their equity from the higher property values. They paid off credit card debt, planned exotic vacations, or bought new cars or appliances.

A large infusion of money flowing into the housing market caused property values to soar. States like Arizona, California, Florida, and Nevada experienced double-digit growth in housing values. Most states tie the level of property taxes to property values. With property values quickly rising, local governments experienced surges in property tax revenue. They used property taxes to expand the police and fire departments, build new jails, libraries, and schools, and hire more teachers.

U.S. politicians did nothing to stem this. They were happy that banks granted anyone a mortgage. Unfortunately, affordable housing remained far from their minds or, worse yet, how poor homeowners could afford to pay higher mortgage payments when they reset to higher interest rates.

The U.S. mortgage party ended in 2007. International investors questioned the financial health of their CDOs, and they turned off the spigot of investment funding. In December 2007, the United States entered the Great Recession, which started the hemorrhaging of jobs.

Homeowners with ARM mortgages saw their interest rates reset to higher levels, making their monthly payments unaffordable. Thus, more homeowners declared bankruptcy as foreclosures began soaring. Consequently, foreclosed homes flooded the real estate market, causing home values to plummet. Some homeowners even fled because their mortgages became worth more than the home's value. Thus, neighborhoods become infested with deserted, boarded-up houses attracting squatters. Squatting led to the growth of a new industry as squatting companies patrolled neighborhoods to drive the settlers out.

Bankruptcy and foreclosure rates continued soaring during 2010. Unfortunately, the exotic securities created several legal problems for foreclosures.

> **Problem 1:** Who has a legal right to foreclose on a home if the borrower defaults? The bank sold the mortgage to the fund and transferred ownership to the mortgage fund. Technically, the fund investors own the home, although the bank manages the fund. Moreover, who has the legal right to renegotiate the terms of a mortgage? Some homeowners thought they had renegotiated lower mortgage payments to the bank. Then the investors foreclosed on their homes because they did not agree to the new mortgage terms.

> **Problem 2:** Banks sometimes misplaced or lost the mortgage paperwork. Thus, some homeowners challenged banks in court and made the banks prove they owned the mortgages. Some homeowners use this technique to delay a foreclosure, or if they are lucky and the bank loses the

paperwork, they could renegotiate a mortgage with more favorable terms.

> ➤ **Problem 3:** Some homeowners bought investment homes with mortgages and rented these properties to tenants. All states differ in their eviction laws. For instance, what would happen to the renters if they paid their rent in full but the landlords defaulted on their mortgages? President Obama fixed this problem by passing a new federal law, the Protecting Tenants at Foreclosure Act.

Companies can utilize CDOs for fraudulent purposes. For example, a company's financial statements look terrible because the company accumulated too much debt on the books. Then the company packages its debt into a CDO and other companies' debt. Then the company becomes an investor and buys into the CDO, converting a debt into an asset. Thus, companies can improve their financial statements using smoke and mirrors. We do not know how many companies artificially used CDOs to inflate their financial statements.

Credit Default Swaps (CDS)

Here is where the story becomes crazier. Some insurance companies and investment banks created Credit Default Swaps (CDS), a type of insurance. For example, some investors want to purchase risky securities because they pay higher returns. However, if a business goes bankrupt, these securities become worthless, and the investors lose their money. Thus, CDSs were born.

Investors could buy risky securities, including Collateralized Debt Obligations and Credit Default Swaps. Investors pay the insurance premium to the investment banks and insurance companies. If a company goes bankrupt and its risky securities collapse in value, the investment bank or insurance company subsequently pays the investors their loss, the CDS contract specifies. If a company with risky securities does not go bankrupt, the investment banks and insurance companies keep the premium payments as pure profits.

Investment banks and insurance companies exposed themselves to high risk. During good economic times, companies rarely file for bankruptcy, even risky businesses that issued risky securities. Companies with a triple-A rating have a zero default rate, while risky companies have a default rating of less than 4%. Thus, the investment banks would collect CDS premiums as pure profit.

A recession continually exposes an organization's weaknesses. For example, during the 2001 recession, AAA-rated companies had close to a zero-default rate, while the default rate shot up to 10% for risky securities [9]. As bankruptcies soared and securities lost value, companies can experience staggering losses during a downturn. The most prominent players of Credit Default Swaps were the same companies that the U.S. government bailed out in 2008. Companies included American International Group (AIG), Bank of America, Citibank, Countrywide Home Loans, GMAC (i.e., former subsidiary of General Motors), General Electric Capital, Goldman Sachs, Lehman Brothers, JP Morgan Chase, Merrill Lynch, Morgan Stanley, and Wachovia [10, 11].

CDSs are contracts that investors can buy and sell in the financial markets. Anyone can buy them, even if the investors do not own the risky bonds specified in the CDS contract. Therefore, speculators can enter the market and gamble on outcomes. For example, a gambler believes Company XYZ is bankrupting. This gambler holds no stock or bonds for this company but can buy a CDS contract. A gambler only pays the CDS premiums. However, if this company does indeed go bankrupt, the gambler gets a payout from the issuer of the CDS contract. If Company XYZ does not go bankrupt, then the gambler has lost his bet, which is the CDS premiums. Imagine how much money someone could make if they possessed inside information about a company's finances. Some investors even bet the housing market would collapse and bought CDS contracts on CDOs [11]. If we have trouble understanding them, then think of this analogy. We have purchased insurance on our neighbor's house and pray the house burns down to collect the insurance.

Finance companies can stack Credit Default Swaps upon each other. For example, Company X buys a CDS contract from an insurance company and pays 2% of the contract's value as a premium. Then the financial health of the company, specified in the CDS contract, deteriorates, increasing the risk on its securities. Company X can exploit this situation by creating and selling a new CDS contract to Company Y for a 6% premium, earning a 4% commission. If that company does indeed go bankrupt, then the insurance company pays Company X its CDS insurance. Company X pays Company Y the same insurance, earning a quick 4% commission on the deal. Thus, multiple CDS contracts cover the same debt. Unfortunately, the CDS contracts depend on a critical assumption. Issuing companies can pay off the CDS contracts if the companies fail.

The CDS market quickly grew to $47 trillion by June 2008, covering a debt of approximately $34 trillion [10]. Putting this number into perspective, the size of the U.S. economy was roughly $15 trillion. Consequently, the potential losses exceeded the size of the U.S. economy by three times if all CDS contracts must be paid.

When the U.S. economy entered a recession in December 2007, AIG quickly accumulated losses into the billions as investors requested the payouts from the CDS contracts. AIG's losses exceeded $60 billion and grew by the day, creating the most significant loss in U.S. corporate history. The U.S. federal government owns 80% equity share [12] and has promised AIG four bailout loans worth $163 billion [13]. Unfortunately, AIG worked with several investment banks like Goldman Sachs and Lehman Brothers, which experienced severe financial troubles. Few news reporters covered this, but AIG thought the U.S. government would bail out Lehman Brothers. Therefore, it issued Credit Default Swaps in the billions of dollars and thought it would collect massive profits from the CDS premiums. Instead, AIG paid billions in claims as Lehman Brothers went bankrupt while its securities became worthless.

Once the public learned that Lehman Brothers was insolvent and the U.S. government would not bail it out[2], the financial markets nosedived in September 2008. Credit markets froze as financial institutions stopped lending. About 350 banks and investors lost their CDS insurance because Lehman Brothers was bankrupted. It issued nearly $400 billion in CDSs on debt valued at $155 billion. Unfortunately, Lehman Brothers issued more CDS contracts than the debt amount by 2.5 times [14].

Lehman Brothers became the most significant casualty of the 2008 Financial Crisis and the largest bankruptcy in U.S. history. Barclays, the second-largest bank in England, bought Lehman Brother's core assets for $1.3 billion, including its skyscraper in Manhattan [15]. Excessive greed destroyed a 158-year-old company.

We list the status of the largest U.S. financial institutions caught in the economic crisis:

> The U.S. federal government helped JP Morgan Chase acquire Bear Stearns [16] and Washington Mutual. Washington Mutual held roughly $52.9 billion in adjustable-rate mortgages [17]. The U.S. Treasury purchased $25 billion in preferred stock [18, 19].

> Bank of America acquired Merrill Lynch and Countrywide Financial Corp. Countrywide held about $25.4 billion in mortgages [17]. Bank of America planned to lay off 30,000 and 35,000 employees [20]. Bank of America received $45 billion from the U.S. Treasury and requested an additional $20 billion. The U.S. Treasury purchased $25 billion in preferred stock [19, 21]. In 2009, Bank of America repaid the $45 billion government loan and earned a quarterly profit of 3.2 billion in July. However, BoA earned the profits from

---

[2]Henry Paulson, Secretary of the U.S. Treasury in 2008, showed the U.S. government would not bail out all the financial institutions. At least one company had to fail, which was Lehman Brothers. However, the Lehman Brothers' collapse spread to other financial institutions like a contagion. Henry Paulson had a possible conflict of interest because he was CEO of Bears Sterns, which fiercely competed with Lehman Brothers.

one-time sources, such as selling its stake in a large Chinese bank [22].

➤ Citigroup Inc. bought Wachovia, which held $122 billion in adjustable-rate mortgages [17]. Moreover, Citigroup planned to lay off up to 19,000 employees [23]. The U.S. government purchased $45 billion in preferred stock, and Citigroup planned to repay $20 billion to the U.S. government. Recently, the federal government converted some of the preferred stock into common stock, giving the U.S. government a 34% stake in the corporation [24].

➤ Deutsche Bank reported a 3.9 billion euro loss [25], its first financial loss in 50 years.

➤ U.S. Treasury purchased $25 billion in preferred stock in Wells Fargo and 10 billion each for Goldman Sachs and Morgan Stanley [19].

➤ The U.S. Treasury invested $19.4 billion in General Motors (GM). However, GM filed for bankruptcy in June 2009. The government may spend another $30 billion to help GM restructure. Meanwhile, GM sales dropped by 45% in 2009 while the company closed plants and discontinued product lines like Pontiac, Saturn, and Hummer. GM plans to lay off 20,000 workers [26].

➤ The federal government owns a 36% stake in GMAC and invested $12.5 billion in two loans [27]. Furthermore, GM sold its interest in GMAC, and Cerberus Capital became the majority shareholder, while the U.S. federal government became second.

Conclusion

Exotic securities depend on a strong, growing U.S. economy. Mortgage default rates remain low while few companies file for bankruptcy. Thus, many U.S. financial companies reaped substantial profits. However, business cycle oscillations plague all market economies. The United States experiences a recession roughly every ten years. It had a recession in 2007, 2001, 1991, and 1981. Nevertheless, these financial geniuses on Wall Street ignored this simple fact as they overextended themselves and their companies for short-term profits.

The Federal Reserve and the U.S. government should share the blame. They should have slowed down the housing bubble. The Federal Reserve could raise interest rates, which would slow the growth of new mortgages. The federal government could impose regulations on exotic securities or tighten lending practices. Unfortunately, Freddie Mac paid $11.7 million to lobbyists, who persuaded Congress to loosen lending standards on the mortgage industry [28]. Consequently, the federal government wanted universal homeownership for all Americans at any cost.

Financial bailouts of large banks and Wall Street came at a high cost. In October 2007, President Bush offered a $700 billion bailout package to the financial system; President Obama offered a $787 billion bailout package to jumpstart the U.S. economy, while the Federal Reserve granted at least $2 trillion in loans to the banking industry. Unfortunately, the Federal Reserve does not publicly release company names because investors would panic.

The public views the government's bailout as free money, so everyone stands in line for a cut. For example, GMAC and two investment banks, Goldman Sachs and Morgan Stanley, became bank holding companies. Thus, they asked the Federal Reserve for emergency loans. Whether these companies can repay these loans is debatable because they earned substantial losses.

The advantages of the bailout package include the following:

> **Advantage 1:** Bailout may slow down the collapse of large financial institutions and provide national and international confidence in the U.S. financial markets. The financial sector represents an important sector of the economy by linking the savers to the borrowers. If savers hoard and bury their money in their backyards, they remove money from the

economy. If the savers deposit this money into financial institutions, then the financial institutions inject this money into the economy, putting the money to work.

> **Advantage 2:** Many households have pension plans linked to the financial market's performance. Although many pension plans took a severe hit, it could be much worse if the government allowed the financial institutions to fail.

Problems of the bailout include the following:

> **Problem 1:** No one bailed out the investors who bought the exotic securities. However, some investors protected their investments by purchasing Credit Default Swaps. They remain protected as long as the issuers can pay their obligations.

> **Problem 2:** The bailout package rewards the financial industry for bad decisions. Monetary companies should be punished. If the U.S. government bails them out, then the government should buy the toxic debt and toxic mortgages for a fraction of their book value, forcing companies to take a loss. If companies know the government will always bail them out, then these companies will always take excessive risks.

> **Problem 3:** Several large banks caught in the crisis should fail because they mistreat their customers. Banks charge excessively high fees and misrepresent loan conditions. For example, a bank applies the charges and withdrawals first to a person's checking account and then applies the deposits, hoping the checking account becomes negative. Next, the bank charges the consumer excessive fees if the account goes negative.

> **Problem 4:** Financial institutions guaranteed too many Credit Default Swaps (CDS) that exceeded the size of the

U.S. economy several times. A bailout package comprises a minuscule drop of water compared to a potential flood of CDS payouts.

> **Problem 5:** The bailout was to get financial institutions to lend again. Unfortunately, the banks hoarded the bailout money and this money does not enter the U.S. economy.

> **Problem 6:** Inflation could become a problem. The U.S. government and Federal Reserve System have injected trillions of dollars into the banking system. If the banks begin lending this money, they inject cash into the economy that will create inflation.

> **Problem 7:** Government programs require homeowners to default before they can get help. Homeowners in financial trouble are incentivized to default on their mortgages so the government can bail them out, too.

> **Problem 8:** The U.S. government has gained ownership in the financial industry. Bureaucrats make terrible decisions and are slow, bureaucratic, and perpetuate complex rules. Moreover, if the U.S. economy enters a decade-long recession like Japan, the U.S. government could accumulate significant losses from holding these financial assets that are losing their value over time.

> **Problem 9:** The bailout could further weaken the U.S. dollar. The bailout had added trillions to the U.S. government debt, and some international investors worry about the government's ability to repay its debt.

A bright spot emerged through the stormy clouds of the 2007 Great Recession. Families are coming together. Kids returned to live with their parents, or the parents moved in with their kids. Furthermore, some couples postpone divorce because they cannot sell the house and divide the marital assets. Finally, economic hard times like the Great Depression produced great leaders. The 2007 Great Recession will make strong leaders who will lead the United States into the next century as a world power.

References

[1] DiLorenzo, Thomas J. September 6, 2007. "The Government-Created Subprime Mortgage Meltdown." *LewRockwell*. Available at http://www.lewrockwell.com/dilorenzo/dilorenzo125.html (access date 02/25/09).

[2] Lotterman, Edward. November 3, 2008. "Lotterman: Blame meltdown on Fannie, Freddie, federal policies." *Idaho Statesman*. Available at http://www.idahostatesman.com/business/story/556667.html?ref=patrick.net (access date 03/03/09).

[3] Schulzke, Kurt. September 26, 2008. "Hidden Clinton "Success Story": Fannie Mae subprime loans for minorities." *Contraries*. http://iperceive.net/hidden-clinton-success-storyfannie- mae-subprime-loans-for-minorities/ (access date 02/25/09).

[4] Charles, Deborah. April 22, 2009. "Freddie Mac CFO in apparent suicide: police source." *Reuters*.

[5] Liu, Betty and Matthew Leising. December 31, 2009. "U.S. to Lose $400 Billion on Fannie, Freddie, Wallison Says." *Business Week*. Available at http://www.businessweek.com/news/2009-12-31/u-s-to-lose-400-billion-on-fannie-freddie-wallison-says.html?source=patrick.net (access date 01/04/2010).

[6] Swann, Christopher and Pimm Fox. September 7, 2008. "U.S. Losses on Fannie, Freddie May Be $300 Billion, Poole Says." *Bloomberg*. Available at http://www.bloomberg.com/apps/news?pid=20601087&refer=patrick.net&sid=aCGy_.UswSS0 (access date 02/26/09).

[7] Rosen, Richard J. November 2007. "The role of securitization in mortgage lending." *Chicago Fed Letter*. Available at http://www.chicagofed.org/publications/fedletter/cflnovember2007_244.pdf (access date 02/22/09).

[8] Rozeff , Michael S. December 26, 2008. "Rating the Rating Agencies and Securitization." *LewRockwell*. Available at http://www.lewrockwell.com/rozeff/rozeff250.html?ref=patrick.net (access date 303/09).

[9] Hamilton, David T., Praveen Varma, Sharon Ou, and Richard Cantor. January 2004. "Default & Recovery Rates of Corporate Bond Issuers.' Moody's Investors Services.

[10] Bajaj, Vikas. November 4, 2008. "Surprises in a Closer Look at Credit-Default Swaps." *The York Times*. Available at

http://www.nytimes.com/2008/11/05/business/05swap.html?_r=1&ref=patrick.net (access date 3/3/09).

[11] Morrissey, Janet. March 17, 2008. "Credit Default Swaps: The Next Crisis?" *Time*. Available at http://www.time.com/time/business/article/0,8599,1723152,00.html (access date 03/04/09).

[12] Karnitschnig, Matthew, Deborah Solomon, Liam Pleven, and Jon E. Hilsenrath. September 16, 2008. "U.S. to Take Over AIG in $85 Billion Bailout; Central Banks Inject Cash as Credit Dries Up." *The Wall Street Journal*. Available at http://online.wsj.com/article/SB122156561931242905.html (access date 03/03/09).

[13] *Dow Jones Newswires*. March 3, 2009. "THE FED: Bernanke Feels Heat From AIG Bailout." Dow Jones & Company. Available at http://money.cnn.com/news/newsfeeds/articles/djf500/200903031154DOW JONESDJONLINE000537_FORTUNE5.htm (access date 03/03/09).

[14] Bawden, Tom and Suzy Jagger. October 11, 2008. "Lehman Brothers demise triggers huge default." *The Times*. Available athttp://business.timesonline.co.uk/tol/business/industry_sectors/banking_and_finance/article4922981.ece?ref=patrick.net (access date 02/26/08).

[15] *BBC News*. September 20, 2008. "Judge approves $1.3bn Lehman deal." Available at http://news.bbc.co.uk/2/hi/business/7626624.stm (access date: 01/04/2010).

[16] Merced, Michael J. de la, Vikas Bajaj and Andrew Ross Sorkin. September 21, 2008. "As Goldman and Morgan Shift, a Wall St. Era Ends." *The New York Times*. Available at http://dealbook.blogs.nytimes.com/2008/09/21/goldman-morgan-to-become-bankholding-companies/?hp&ref=patrick.net (access date 02/26/09).

[17] Ivry, Bob. September 29, 2008. "Wachovia's `Great Success' Became $122 Billion Burden." *Bloomberg*. Available at http://www.bloomberg.com/apps/news?pid=20601109&sid=aebs.K1QUWTo&refer=patrick.net (access date 2/26/09).

[18] Kiel, Paul. February 5, 2009. "Report: Treasury Collects $271 Million in Dividends on Bailout." *ProPublica*. Available at http://www.propublica.org/article/report-treasury-collects-271- million-in-dividends-on-bailout (access date 03/05/09).

[19] Special Inspector General. February 6, 2009. "Office of the Special Inspector General for the Troubled Asset Relief Program." *Initial Report to Congress*. Available at http://s3.amazonaws.com/propublica/assets/docs/sigtarp_090205.pdf (access date 03/05/09).

[20] Weiss, Tara. December 16, 2008. "Bank Of America Is Doing Layoffs All Wrong." *Forbes*. Available at http://www.forbes.com/2008/12/16/bank-

america-layoff leadershipgovernance-cx_tw_1215bofa.html (access date 03/05/09).

[21] Mildenberg, David. March 3, 2009. "Bank of America Downgraded by Standard & Poor's." *Bloomberg*. Available at http://www.bloomberg.com/apps/news?pid=20601087&sid=aWu38qrgIbjQ &refer=home (access date 03/05/09).

[22] *The New York Times*. December 17, 2009. "Bank of America Corporation." Available at http://topics.nytimes.com/top/news/business/companies/bank_of_america_c orporation/index.html (access date: 01/05/2010).

[23] Ellis, David and Aaron Smith. November 14, 2008. "Citigroup to lay off another 10,000 – report." *CNN Money*. Available at http://money.cnn.com/2008/11/14/news/companies/citigroup_layoffs/index. htm?postversion=2008111415 (access date 03/04/09).

[24] Ellis, David. December 14, 2009. "Citigroup strikes deal to repay TARP." *CNN Money*. Available at http://money.cnn.com/2009/12/14/news/companies/citigroup_tarp/ (access date: 01/05/2010).

[25] Investor Relations. February 5, 2009. "Deutsche Bank reports net loss of EUR 3.9 billion for the year 2008." *Deutsche Bank*. Available at http://www.db.com/ir/en/content/ir_releases_2009_7249.htm (access date 02/26/09).

[26] Isidore, Chis. June 2, 2009. "GM bankruptcy: End of an era." *CNN Money*. Available at http://money.cnn.com/2009/06/01/news/companies/gm_bankruptcy/index.ht m (access date: 01/04/2010).

[27] Irwin, Neil and David Cho. May 22, 2009. "As GMAC Gets More Aid, Bailout Becomes One of Nation's Biggest." *The Washington Post*. Available at http://www.washingtonpost.com/wp-dyn/content/article/2009/05/21/AR2009052101742.html (access date 01/04/2010).

[28] *SF Examiner*. December 9, 2008. "Daily Outrage: Mortgage giant paid $11.7 million to lobby Congress." Available at http://www.sfexaminer.com/opinion/Daily_Outrage_Mortgage_giant_paid_ 117_million_ to_lobby_Congress.html?ref=patrick.net (access date 03/03/08).

11. A Grim Future

"I think we have more machinery of government than is necessary, too many parasites living on the labor of the industrious."

-Sir Francis Bacon

Our U.S. legal system is not healthy and does not promote free enterprise. Government at all levels has invaded the lives of families and private businesses as they regulate all aspects of our lives. Here is where the problem lies. The U.S. has created a complex legal system that is far beyond being too complicated for both people and experts. Even experts hire experts to help them understand the law.

Furthermore, the federal, state, and local governments have established a plethora of regulatory agencies to enforce these intricate rules. Regrettably, these enforcers and regulators have become overly zealous and strict, imprisoning individuals and seizing property for the most minor infractions of the law, often for trivial violations.

We, the people, are faced with an unmanageable government. This poses a significant problem, as the government should be streamlining programs, reducing bureaucracies, and controlling spending. However, at all levels, the government is doing the opposite, expanding bureaucracies, increasing taxes, and further complicating our laws.

An overbearing, monstrous government threatens and destroys society. This simple premise is easy to prove. Look at the 2007 Great Recession; the U.S. economy is still sputtering in 2012, and the recession continues unabated.

We observe the last three recessions. Economists call the 1991 recession the Jobless Recovery. The U.S. economy recovered but did not create jobs as our society left that recession. We call the 2001 recession the Job-Loss Recovery. The U.S. economy recovered, but companies and corporations continued shedding jobs and laying people off. Now, we experienced the 2007 Great Recession with a non-existent recovery.

If we went back to 1961, we had a recession that lasted one year. The recession was only a bump in the road, and subsequently, the

U.S. economy recovered and moved ahead at full steam. Since every recession, economic recovery has become weaker and weaker. Which trends would cause weaker recoveries since 1961? Technological change, bigger government, and the decline of ethics and morality. Which entity would we blame for our continued stagnation?

Perpetual Bear Financial Markets

People and businesses using a first line of defense against an intrusive, cash-hungry government will use more cash transactions. Cash transactions do not create third-party records. For instance, if a business uses a check to pay its bill, its bank becomes a third party to this transaction and maintains a record. Subsequently, government can use bank records to piece together a person's income and wealth. Consequently, the government cannot verify a person's or business's income if they use cash transactions.

Cash transactions can protect people against lawyers because lawyers do background searches on people before initiating a lawsuit. Why would a lawyer sue a person if he appears to have no money? Thus, more businesses and people will avoid paying their taxes, or they protect themselves from lawsuits using cash transactions.

Several states and European countries outlawed cash transactions. For example, Louisiana banned cash transactions for second-hand sales, while Spain prohibits all cash transactions above 2,500 euros. The government wants to collect tax revenue, even if it hikes taxes to unreasonable levels. Finally, many states require workers receiving unemployment benefits or other state aid to use debit cards that create third-party records.

Holding large amounts of cash is dangerous. People and businesses using a second line of defense can move their wealth to offshore accounts. An offshore account is a bank account in a country with strict, confidential laws, few regulations, and low tax rates. Familiar places include the Bahamas, Cayman Islands, Lichtenstein, and Switzerland.

The problem with offshore accounts is people and businesses can hide income. For example, a person works for a company in the U.S., and all the paperwork indicates this person earns $30,000 per year in taxable income. Nevertheless, the company pays its workers $60,000 using offshore accounts to hide some of their income. The company makes secret bank transfers from its offshore account to that person's offshore account. All the paperwork resides outside the United States and beyond the reach of the tax agents, scum-bag lawyers, and bureaucrats.

The U.S. government worries about tax evasion and has become more insidious about tracking foreign bank accounts. The IRS can scrutinize anyone's credit card information, such as VISA and MasterCard, and check whether people travel to countries with offshore banking. The IRS views these people as potential tax evaders who require closer scrutiny. Furthermore, the U.S. government can pressure these countries to force them to reveal their bank records. Still, a person needs seconds to transfer his funds electronically to another bank in another country. Recently, the IRS and U.S. government prosecutors threatened to incarcerate the top executives of USB, a Swiss Bank, to reveal accounts held by Americans in Switzerland or face lengthy prison sentences.

A cash economy and offshore accounts strain a country's financial markets. People do not invest cash into bank accounts, stocks, bonds, and pension funds within the United States. Financial markets are vital for wealthy countries because they link the savers to the borrowers. People deposit their money into financial institutions. In turn, the financial institutions lend the funds to borrowers. Borrowers include businesses that use loans to invest in machines and equipment or families that borrow money to buy a house, car, or appliance. Thus, the loans feed the money into the economy and help generate a society's wealth.

If people lose faith in the financial markets and hoard or hide their cash in foreign bank accounts, savers refrain from investing it in the U.S. financial markets. Many people did not deposit their savings into banks during the Great Depression. People hid money in mattresses or buried it in backyards. Unfortunately, they did not invest this money in the U.S. economy.

The U.S. federal government panicked during the 2008 Financial Crisis and offered a bailout package of $700 billion. The purpose of the bailout was to prevent the financial markets from going under. A faltering financial system forces a country into a third-world country. Third-world countries do not develop and become affluent.

The bailout has the following four problems.

> **Problem 1:** Everyone considers this free money, and many institutions stood in line for the handout, such as banks, insurance companies, the automobile industry, school districts, and state governments. Even the porn industry, Larry Flint of Hustler and Joe Francis of "Girls Gone Wild," had asked for a handout [1].

> **Problem 2:** The U.S. government did not provide oversight on the funding. This was unusual because the federal government always imposes authority and control over public funding.

> **Problem 3:** The public became enraged over the bailout. Taxpayers believed the government had bailed out companies that made bad investment decisions.

> **Problem 4:** Several companies inappropriately spent the bailout money, fueling the fire. Some companies used the bailout money to buy other banks, pay bonuses to high-ranking executives, or hoard the money. Remember, the government gave the bailout money to get banks to start lending again, not hold onto it!

Many financial analysts do not talk about the retiring baby boomers. For stock prices to keep increasing, people must continually invest funds into the stock market. However, as the baby boomers retire, they will cash out their stock portfolios. Hence, the U.S. stock markets could be a poor investment because the baby boomers retire and withdraw their savings from financial markets.

Then compound this problem with people hiding their money from the government, lawyers, and bureaucrats.

Fleeing Businesses

Businesses are fleeing the United States and relocating to Asia and Mexico. Many experts cite the cheap labor in China and Mexico. However, no one mentions the punitive legal environment in the United States that results from excessive regulations, frivolous lawsuits, and high taxes. They boost the cost of doing business in the United States. Then coupled with the high costs and high wage rates, the U.S. has a crushing business environment. A company operating in the United States must pay:

> **Income Taxes:** A business may pay federal, state, county, and city income taxes. Income taxes vary by state and locality. A company with several branches in different states requires a department to keep track of the other rules, regulations, and taxes.

> **Property Taxes:** In some cities, property taxes are quite high, especially for capital-intensive industries such as computer chip and automobile industries. Many people do not realize this, but many localities assess taxes on machines and equipment. Thus, the manufacturing industry pays high property tax bills, which encourages it to relocate overseas.

> **Social Security and Medicare Taxes:** The federal government collects these taxes from the employer and employee. Workers pay roughly 6% of their wages to Social Security and 1% to Medicare. The employer matches the dollar amount of the taxes that the employees pay.

> **Workers' Disability Insurance:** State governments dictate the insurance rates. This insurance is not voluntary. Therefore, we should view it as a tax because a business transfers money from itself to the government. Furthermore,

many young people are inflicted with disabilities and do not work. Unfortunately, it is difficult to assess whether the person is disabled or pretending to be disabled to receive a monthly check.

➢ **Unemployment Insurance:** State governments set the rates for unemployment insurance. This insurance is not voluntary because employers must pay it. Unlike workers' disability, unemployed workers receive this aid temporarily, at least theoretically. For the 2007 Great Recession, some laid-off people successfully collected unemployment for 99 weeks (almost two years). They call them the 99 Club because Congress kept extending the time for unemployment insurance for states stuck in the recession.

➢ **Medical Insurance and Pension Plans:** Employers must offer full-time workers medical insurance and contribute to employees' pension funds. The key word is full-time, which is why some employers in the services industry rely on part-time workers.

➢ **Unfunded Mandates:** Federal, state, and local governments impose numerous mandates on businesses. The government dictates a rule or regulation but does not pay for it.

➢ **Lawsuits:** Attorneys continually attack the medical and pharmaceutical industries. Lawsuits can add millions to a company's loss.

Governments in Asian countries do not subject their businesses to all these insurance programs and taxes. Furthermore, lawsuits are rare, and regulations are lax. Chinese workers earn a meager $10 per day for 12 hours of work, and the Chinese companies ship the products to the United States.

The decline of manufacturing in the U.S. became so devastating that scrap metal dealers loaded barges with scrap metal and shipped it to China. Then Chinese factories produced finished products that U.S. companies shipped to the U.S.

How does the United States government reward businesses and help them to thrive and grow? The U.S. government passed universal health care and a permit system for greenhouse gas emissions. Healthcare plans caused massive uncertainty, and employers stopped hiring workers, creating a terrible job market in 2012. Then the permit system requires firms emitting greenhouse gases to buy permits. Thus, these two recent laws will hurl more hardship and costs onto our businesses. Consequently, the government encourages more U.S. businesses to flee, produce in foreign countries, and export their products to the United States.

Fleeing businesses cause a severe problem. If businesses leave the United States, who employs the workers? With tax revenues decreasing and governments at all levels experiencing severe budget deficits, the government would stop hiring. Therefore, the U.S. unemployment rate continually rises over time. Margaret Thatcher summed this up best by saying, "First, we produce. Then we consume." Asian countries know this secret well and continue growing, even after the 2008 Financial Crisis. In 2012, China's economy grew phenomenally at 10% per year.

Fleeing businesses also lead to underinvestment in our society. High taxes, fees, fines, regulations, and lawsuits create a punitive legal environment that does not encourage new investments. Consequently, businesses extract every penny they can from their capital and refuse to update their machines, equipment, and infrastructure. For example, a natural gas line ruptured and exploded in California, killing four people. Several oil platforms in the Gulf of Mexico erupted into flames, including the infamous British Petroleum oil well that spewed almost a million gallons of crude oil into the Gulf of Mexico.

The government does not invest in the economy. It worries about locking people up than replacing old, outdated, and dilapidated bridges, roads, and other infrastructure. For instance, a bridge collapsed in Minnesota, and several dams were on the verge of collapsing during torrential rain storms in the Midwest. Consequently, the government underinvests in our society.

We constructed most of our infrastructure during the 1940s and 1950s. Over time, more accidents will occur as our infrastructure continues aging and crumbling while businesses and governments refuse to invest in our society.

Excessively Enforcing the Laws

A large, intrusive government requires funding that it collects from the taxpayers. With a punitive legal system, people will hide their money and income from the government. Businesses could go bankrupt, relocate to a foreign country, violate the law, or evade taxes. All these activities cause a loss of tax revenue for the government. An eroding tax base hurts government finance, which imposes the following costs on society:

> **Cost 1:** As tax revenues continually decline, a government must contract. How can the government pay for the army of bureaucrats, jails, prisons, and government buildings if it has no money? The government does finance good institutions, such as libraries, schools, universities, and parks. These institutions would experience severe budget problems as our leaders reduce funding for these programs. Usually, the government funds these good institutions last.

> **Cost 2:** An eroding tax base may cause our government to pass more laws to create more violators. Then the state and courts would depend on the police and regulators to write tickets and citations, bringing money into the government coffers. For example, code enforcement officers may comb through middle-class neighborhoods and measure grass height, citing any offenders for too-tall grass. However, these same officers avoid the poor neighborhoods because those citizens may not pay the fines and may attack the officers. Thus, the legal system becomes more arbitrary as it seeks revenue.

> **Cost 3:** If the government actually contracts, this would create a power vacuum, and criminal groups like the mafia would fill this void. The mafia will supply products, which could be legal or illegal. As the mafia accumulates money and wealth, it pays off the police, judges, and bureaucrats. If the police and prosecutors are not corrupt, they have few resources to do their jobs well.

Police officers must follow orders from the government, or the government leaders will fire them. For police to do their jobs, they take an "us versus them" mentality. Each time a police officer clocks in, they battle with the public. That is why they call every person of interest a criminal. The Military uses the same mentality to train soldiers by defining the enemy as subhuman. Thus, soldiers can handle the intense emotions of war and killing people. Some long-run consequences of excessive enforcement of the laws include the following:

> **Consequence 1:** The government relies on violators to pay for their tickets and citations. As police write more citations and enforce stupid laws, more people will become scofflaws and not pay them. The government will increase court and police power to seize assets and turn decent citizens into criminals. For example, a person refused to pay for his ticket for a violation he did not do. A court could suspend his driver's license or other licenses. The legal right to drive a car in our society is a necessary privilege, so he may start driving illegally, not insure his vehicle legally, and stop paying for car inspections and state car tags. Furthermore, this person may drive junky cars on the road if he knows the police will seize his vehicle when caught. Overzealous enforcement of laws creates more criminals and scofflaws.

> **Consequence 2:** More people will avoid the police. Would we call the police or open the door for the police if we knew they were there to write tickets and citations? Remember, the police are the first contact with a government starving for

cash. The government switched the role of police from public safety to revenue thugs with guns. Even in Arkansas, citizens flash their car headlights twice to warn oncoming traffic that police are farther up the road.

➤ **Consequence 3:** Police and courts rely on the public for information. If many people regard their government in low regard and do not trust it, they will not help it. For example, if a citizen discovers that someone has vandalized police cars, the citizen may not report it.

➤ **Consequence 4:** The police lose their credibility during jury trials. Many people will learn the police will lie, even for minor things such as traffic citations. Police officers must write citations and arrest people to keep their quotas up. That is why the federal and state governments rewrote laws to move away from jury trials.

➤ **Consequence 5:** Court abuse will become greater and bolder as the economy remains in recession. Tax collections continue plummeting while many states and local governments go broke. Thus, courts will collect as much money as they can as judges declare all defendants guilty!

The government passing stupid laws and excessively enforcing laws will fuel ill will and bitterness between the people and the government. Consequently, more people will attack their government. They can vandalize state property or physically harm the police or bureaucrats. For example, an arsonist set the Texas Governor's Mansion on fire, causing severe damage [2]. This book does not advocate that people should start attacking their government. The author merely presents long-term consequences when the government fosters an abusive relationship between the government and its citizens.

Growing Crime and Black Markets

Black markets flourish in highly regulated and over-taxed societies. A black market is where people engage in illegal activities, and it exists for the following reasons:

> **Reason 1:** The government deems certain products and services illegal. Unfortunately, as the government makes more products and services illegal, black markets expand. If consumers demand illicit products and services, then somebody will supply them. That is the flaw with the War on Drugs. The U.S. and state governments deemed marijuana use illegal. As the government arrests more drug dealers, marijuana supplies dwindle, which boosts the market price. Then the high prices attract more people to this illegal market as more people become drug dealers.

> **Reason 2:** People and businesses use black markets to avoid laws and regulations. For example, some workers circumvent retirement restrictions. Retired people receive Social Security and other government benefits but work "under the table" for extra income. If the government knew about this income, it would reduce their benefits. Another example is foreign laborers working illegally in this country using fake names and Social Security Numbers [3].

> **Reason 3:** People use black markets to avoid high taxes. One method is barter, when two people trade goods or services with each other, and they do not exchange money. Thus, they place no value on the transaction and pay no taxes. Other ways to avoid high taxes are people and businesses underreporting income and assets or overstating debt. For example, taxpayers in the United States can claim children on U.S. federal taxes. More children mean lower taxes. Before the 1990s, some people claimed their pets as children to reduce taxes. People no longer get away with this practice unless their pet has a Social Security Number.

Regulations and taxes cause people to perceive their government overburdens them, so they operate in the shadow economy. (Black markets, shadow economy, and hidden economy mean the same thing). However, a growing shadow economy imposes costs on society:

> **Cost 1:** A growing shadow economy leads to more corruption and bribery because individuals who engage in illegal activity will bribe public officials. Thus, they can avoid regulations or avoid paying taxes.

> **Cost 2:** A growing shadow economy erodes the tax base, so the government has fewer resources to invest in infrastructure and education. Furthermore, an eroding tax base may cause a government to hike taxes, forcing firms and individuals to enter the shadow economy and creating a vicious cycle. Many businesses and people who evade their taxes may be good for governments that incarcerate a large percentage of their population. Thus, the government does not have the funding to incarcerate people.

> **Cost 3:** The government collects statistical data, which may be inaccurate. For example, if people work "under the table," they may lie to the government and say they are working. Consequently, the unemployment statistics would be higher than reality. Some people working under the table receive money from disability or unemployment insurance.

> **Cost 4:** A growing shadow economy expands the criminal groups because they thrive in highly taxed and regulated economies. That is what criminals do; they violate the rules and laws.

> **Cost 5:** The government must build and expand prisons to incarcerate violators and criminals.

Declining Civic Loyalty and Growing Political Corruption

The rapid rise in the State causes people to give up on the political system. The government expands as its bureaucrats make more decisions. Consequently, the only things growing in the economy are taxes, regulations, and bureaucrats' salaries. For instance, if we are the freest people in the world, why do half the eligible voters vote? Furthermore, a 2002 survey showed that 43% of people in the U.S. have no or little trust in the government, with the highest distrust being the young and elderly [4]. Conversely, 57% of the population trusts the government, which seems low since we are a democracy.

Many people view their government negatively. These opinions do not come from criminals and drug dealers. Highly educated people, government employees, and veterans of the armed forces criticize our government.

The most striking criticism of the government comes from veterans, who have defended the country at the risk of their lives. Their potential sacrifice is the highest a person can make, yet they return to a country where they feel compelled to criticize the government. This paradox highlights the issue as people lose faith in their government.

Citizens develop opinions of their government through their daily dealings with it. If a new tax burned a citizen, violated a crazy regulation, or sued for a stupid reason, they would develop harsh views of their government. Moreover, excessive laws and frivolous lawsuits destroy the market system. Incomes and wealth begin falling as the job-creation machine shuts down. As incomes fall, so does the tax revenue. If the government perpetually operates budget deficits, then salaries for judges, police, and bureaucrats will decline. Once wages become too low, more judges will accept bribes to determine who wins a court case. Police will accept cash fines; teachers will take bribes and pass failing students. This is no joke because they became severe problems in Russia after the Soviet Union collapsed.

Black markets became ingrained into the Russian people's psyche, and crime skyrocketed after the Soviet Union broke up in 1991. Mafia, called "new businessmen," spread to all parts of the post-Soviet economy like cancer. The mafia created rackets, where they conspired together to sell products, such as cigarettes, sodas, and other products for high prices and earned huge profits. Then, the mafia would bribe government officials, who would protect the mafia and their businesses.

Foreign companies had trouble entering the Russian markets. For example, a foreign company wants to enter the country and open a new factory. However, the mafia does not want any competition, and they pay off the right people, so this foreign company could never get the licenses and permits to operate. Furthermore, foreign companies must follow all the rules because the Russian government will expel them for any violation. Unfortunately, their local competitors may not follow all the rules, giving them a cost and price advantage. Hence, the post-Soviet economies became riddled with criminal groups while consumers paid high prices for everything.

Once corruption has taken root, it grows into a vicious weed that is hard to eliminate. Widespread corruption creates two problems. First, the government has more trouble stopping corruption. If all the public officials take bribes and steal, who will stand up and stop this, especially if this person is also stealing? This is one of the significant problems in cleaning up corruption in Louisiana. Most political leaders steal and want to avoid drawing attention to themselves. Second, people lose respect for their government institutions. Thus, taxpayers do not feel bad when they cheat or lie on their tax returns. They believe the government will waste and squander their hard-earned money.

The Collapsing U.S. Dollar

The U.S. free trade policies are insidious and continue destroying our country. The correct definition of free trade is when one country makes something and sells it to another country. Then the other country makes something and sells it back to the first country. Thus, both countries produce products and export the excess to other countries.

The United States does not do that. Instead, the government encourages U.S. companies to shut down in the United States and relocate to Asia. Then they specifically produce products that are shipped to the United States. No mutual exchange of goods exists between the countries. Thus, the manufacturing industry creates wealth and jobs outside the United States, although U.S. businesses sell the final products to American consumers. Consequently, U.S. companies can escape the punitive U.S. legal structure and still profit by selling to Americans.

One popular escape for U.S. companies is China. Consequently, China has a quarter of the world's industrial space and is growing phenomenally, with wealth soaring. With all this new wealth, the Chinese government financed a space program and sent an astronaut into outer space.

This is great for the Chinese, but what about the plight of the U.S. workers? Our fellow Americans are losing good-paying factory jobs in the Rust Belt, which includes states like Indiana, Ohio, Michigan, and Wisconsin that experienced massive factory closures. Factory buildings become abandoned and gradually rust away from the elements.

U.S. consumers subsidize the growth of Asian countries like China through trade deficits, which have plagued our country since the 1960s. A trade deficit occurs when U.S. consumers buy more foreign-made goods than what they sell to foreigners, causing U.S. dollars to flow to foreign countries. As foreign governments and investors accumulate these dollars, they have three investment options.

> **Option 1:** Foreign businesses and companies invest in their economies by purchasing machines and equipment from the United States. They spur future economic growth by investing in their economy.

> **Option 2:** Foreign governments and investors can save dollars. Usually, foreign central banks hold strong currencies

like the U.S. dollar, which they can use to manipulate exchange rates. Asian countries weaken their currencies and strengthen the U.S. dollar, which boosts their exports and creates jobs and wealth in Asia.

➢ **Option 3:** Foreign investors can invest the U.S. dollars in the U.S. economy. Asian and Middle Eastern countries buy U.S. government securities, U.S. businesses, and real estate. However, foreigners expect to earn a profit, which means future dollars will flow out of the country again as the foreigners cash in their investments.

With the 2008 Financial Crisis, international investors are rethinking their investments in the U.S. economy. They worry the U.S. federal government has accumulated too much debt, and the 2007 Great Recession may transform into the Second Great Depression. If investors drop the U.S. dollar, its value will collapse.

A weak U.S. dollar has a dual effect. It hurts U.S. consumers by making foreign products more expensive. However, U.S. businesses benefit because they make U.S.-produced goods cheaper to foreigners, who subsequently buy more. A weak U.S. dollar would not jump-start the U.S. manufacturing industry because a weaker dollar would not be strong enough for manufacturing companies to overcome all the problems associated with regulations, taxes, and lawsuits in the U.S.

A collapsing U.S. dollar spells trouble for the U.S. government. Foreign investors and savers hold strong currencies, thus maintaining their investments. If international investors stop holding the U.S. dollar, then the dollar would collapse in value. Consequently, global investors would not invest in the United States and stop buying U.S. government securities. The federal government could not rely on foreigners to finance its massive debt.

Once foreigners stop buying U.S. government securities, the U.S. government must drastically cut its spending. If the U.S. government refuses to control its spending, high inflation will strike the economy as the U.S. government turns to print money to cover its spending. This is why gold soared beyond $1,900 per ounce in

2011. During an economic crisis, investors hold precious metals to protect their wealth from high inflation or hyperinflation.

Which foreign currency would replace the U.S. dollar? The euro was strengthening and gaining value against the U.S. dollar until 2008. However, Europe experienced severe financial troubles after the 2008 Financial Crisis, and the euro quickly lost value. With China still growing, the viable alternative would be the Chinese Yuan. Unfortunately, international trade would halt if the U.S. currency collapsed and no other currency replaced the U.S. dollar. This happened during the Great Depression when the United States government imposed high import tariffs, and all the trade partners reciprocated.

Hyperinflation

The last section was never intended for inclusion in this book. However, it is important to note that hyperinflation's source always originates from a nation's central bank. When the inflation rate surpasses 10% annually, it is typically due to the central bank injecting excessive money into the banking system and economy.

A common scenario is a government has a severe budget deficit. The investors refuse to buy the government's debt. They believe the government's finances will become unstable and do not want to risk their money. For example, Standard & Poor downgraded the U.S. government's credit rating in 2011. Consequently, the government must reduce spending, increase taxes, or use the central bank to print money.

Although the Federal Reserve System remains independent of the U.S. federal government, the federal government could force the Federal Reserve to buy its securities. As the Federal Reserve buys trillions in U.S. securities, it injects trillions of dollars into the banking system and the economy, creating inflation.

High inflation leads to hyperinflation, which has five problems:

> ➤ **Problem 1:** Hyperinflation can have a significant impact on debt and savings. For instance, individuals with debt may find that hyperinflation effectively wipes out their financial

obligations, as the value of money decreases. On the other hand, savers could see their hard-earned money diminish in value.

> **Problem 2:** People who receive aid from the government will experience decreases in their benefits as the prices for food and necessities rise faster than their government aid.

> **Problem 3:** Hyperinflation can also weaken the value of the U.S. dollar on the international stage, potentially leading to a shift in currency preferences. This could disrupt international trade, as countries may opt for alternative currencies for their transactions.

> **Problem 4:** Banks, financial markets, and pension funds will go bankrupt. People stopped accepting U.S. dollars for payment and used barter, foreign currencies, or valuable commodities for exchange.

> **Problem 5:** Police and firefighters may desert their posts as hyperinflation reduces their salaries to nothing. Consequently, violence and chaos could erupt in the cities.

Some experts believe the U.S. hyperinflation will be short because the U.S. government will eliminate its enormous debt, start over, and redefine the U.S. dollar. However, during the interim, hyperinflation will push many people onto the streets as they become homeless and hungry with no prospects. Violent protests and riots could riddle the United States.

Conclusion

The 2008 Financial Crisis and the Great Recession helped the U.S. government to take over the economy. They believe capitalism has failed, and the government must come to the rescue. For example, the federal government re-nationalized Fannie Mae and Freddie Mac in September 2008. They were government public corporations, but the U.S. government had privatized them in the 1990s. With the $700 billion government bailout, the government accepted some of the "toxic mortgages" and corporate stock as collateral. Then the government became a stockholder and foolishly believed it could profit with the taxpayers' money, coming out ahead. However, asset prices took 20 years to recover from the Great Depression after the stock market crashed in 1929.

These intelligent people in government do not realize one crucial thing. They want to improve society through state management of the economy. Another leader, Vladimir Lenin, shared this same vision. Lenin used communism to build the Soviet Union. Communism was a way for a state to make a perfect, Utopian society. Communism would eliminate the social classes, and everyone would live in harmony. Of course, the government must control the entire society, helping during the transition.

The Soviet Union did some fantastic things, which include the following:

> Russia was a backward nation at the turn of the 20th century. The Soviet Union established an extensive education system and boosted its citizens' literacy rate to 99%.

> The Soviet Union officially did not have unemployment. The state created jobs for everyone. Of course, nobody actually worked, and customers shopped in stores with bare shelves.

> The Soviet Union started the space race by sending the first astronaut into outer space.

> Although the Soviet Union was an incredibly sexist society, the state allowed women to hold high offices. Women became judges, professors, and scientists.

> Divorce rates were low because the Soviet Union had a housing shortage. A divorced woman had two choices: to live with her husband or with her parents.

> When the world entered the Great Depression during the 1930s, the downturn did not impact the Soviet economy. The Soviet Union grew fast as the government added and expanded cities to the empire until the 1970s.

The Soviet economy stagnated during the 1970s and 1980s. The citizens of the Soviet Union paid high costs for these benefits, which include the following:

> The government sets all prices and wages in society. The government set the wages and prices correctly during the 1960s, but severe shortages occurred during the 1980s.

> Soviet factories produced only several brands and products. Everyone had the same furniture, appliances, and TVs. Some products suffered quality problems. Soviet managers had production quotas, and they viewed quality as secondary.

> The government-owned all property, including cars and houses. The state forced the people to live in dreary, small apartments.

> The Soviet Union created new social classes. Members of the Communist Party were at the top; scientists and academe came second, and everyone else was third. Communist Party members also shopped at their special stores with fully stocked shelves, while the people shopped at state stores with bare shelves.

> Government-controlled TV stations, newspapers, and book publishing. State-controlled all sources of information.

> The government established secret police, who arrested anyone the state considered a threat. Furthermore, the government constructed a massive prison system, Gulag, to house all the prisoners.

> ➢ When Stalin seized power, he shuffled resources to create the Soviet industrial economy. Thousands died from hunger as the state expropriated lands and livestock. Stalin also executed millions of people whom he deemed a threat to the state.

> ➢ The government restricted the mobility of its citizens. A person needed permission to leave a city. All cities had outposts on the city's periphery, where the state regulated all traffic leaving and entering the city.

> ➢ Soviet citizens could not leave the country nor socialize with foreigners.

Does this sound like a great place to live? Of course, it would be nice to have the Soviet benefits without the costs. However, when the government controls society, we experience the good, the bad, and the ugly of a government-controlled economy.

The absolute travesty in our growing government is the difficulty in dismantling public institutions and reforming the legal system. For instance, remnants of the Soviet legal system still exist today, although the Soviet Union broke up in 1991. The Soviet Union created manual, document-heavy bureaucracies. Corrupt, incompetent bureaucrats enjoy forcing citizens to jump through hoops and legal hurdles. Citizens and businessmen must scurry around the city, collecting documents from various agencies. Unfortunately, the post-Soviet governments want to scrutinize and examine every private transaction in society.

Although the Soviet legal system is beautiful in theory, it successfully killed businesses. Unfortunately, many former Soviet countries are still plagued with these bureaucracies and the Soviet legal system. Then people wonder why these countries experience little growth. The real problem for us is that U.S. politicians want a system similar to that of an all-controlling government. Thus, the U.S. economy will continue to stagnate until people wake up and stop this insanity! However, we will fall into the same trap as Russia.

Once the government creates these laws and the bureaucracies come to life, they are hard to eliminate and reform.

References

[1] Hill, Catey. January 7, 2009. "Porn kings Larry Flint and Joe Francis go begging for a bailout." *Daily News*. Available at http://www.nydailynews.com (access date 01/08/09).
[2] Robison, Clay and Janet Elliot. June 8, 2008. "Arson suspected at Governor's Mansion." *Houston Chronicle*.
[3] Schneider, Friedrich and Dominik H. Enste. March 2000. "Shadow Economies: Size, Causes, and Consequences." *Journal of Economic Literature* 38(1): 77-114.
[4] *Decision Analyst*. August 30, 2002. "As September 11th Anniversary Nears More Americans Trust U.S. government." Available at http://www.decisionanalyst.com/publ_data/2002/trust.dai (access date: 12/24/08).

I was born in a small town in Michigan, filled with the noises of factories. While growing up, I witnessed factory closures, which brought high unemployment and few economic prospects. I left the town to pursue my dreams and enrolled in a university. My education opened the door to the world, where I graduated with a Ph.D. in environmental and natural resource economics from Texas A&M University. With my degree, I traveled and lived in Bosnia and Herzegovina, the Republic of Kazakhstan, Morocco, Malaysia, and the United States. Currently, I teach economics and finance at a small university in Morocco. Despite my humble beginnings as a poor boy from Michigan, I am doing alright. I am living life to the fullest.

Other books from the author:

The Arduous Path to Enlightenment

As human beings, we often ponder upon our existence on this earth and ask ourselves why we are here. We search for answers through various religions like Hinduism, Buddhism, Christianity, Islam, and Judaism. They share a common theme where God wants us to use all our talents and become closer to Him. We examine methods like fasting, meditation, lucid dreaming, sensory deprivation, and mind-altering drugs such as psychedelics and marijuana to explore our minds and awaken our spirituality. We delve into the deep depths of our minds and psyches to gain greater awareness and uncover hidden aspects of ourselves. Through this journey, we discover our true selves and purpose in life while traversing the path to enlightenment.

My Journey into the World of Intermittent Fasting

Intermittent fasting is a journey with many twists and turns. We may not be exploring ancient stone ruins in the jungles of Cambodia or savoring the exotic flavors of spicy Thai cuisine from the food carts on the streets of Bangkok. However, fasting is a journey to a healthier body. In this book, I take you on this journey, sharing practical insights and tips on all aspects of fasting. I've distilled my knowledge and extensive research into an easy-to-follow guide, including 50 practical tips on fasting, exercise, and nutrition. My book is a tool that can help you discover the power of intermittent fasting and unlock the doors to a healthy, long life.

Paying for College – The Novel

Brothers, I only wanted to attend a university and escape a small town with no job prospects or future. But every time I opened my mailbox at the dorm, I pulled out another tuition bill with a looming due date. So, I had to do the unthinkable—break a few rules and do some insane things. Then everything just became crazy.

To Tame Man

The United Federation of Cities has been at peace since the Great War, and one of its great cities, Chicago, has experienced no violence, no crime, and no murders in 68 years. Then Susan, the director of the Male Processing Unit, ran out of Growth Inhibitor 37, and several males, including Brown 447, didn't get their treatment. Unfortunately, Brown 447 shows an uncanny intelligence and rises up and challenges the society of Chicago. Mayor Lilith and the Mayor's Guards must restore the social order and return law and order to Chicago.

Searching for Stolen Love

I'm an American finance professor who was excited to teach at the Bosnian University of Management, located in the heartland of Bosnia and Herzegovina. I went there to make a difference, and my future was looking bright. I fell in love with a Serbian woman and had just finished teaching my first semester. But one winter night, my girlfriend had disappeared, and no one could help me. I searched for her and unraveled quite a mystery in the land of blood and honey.

The Second American Revolution – The Building of an Empire

As a child, Jerrick Ray Davis dreamed of delivering powerful speeches to the people. He also dreams of building an Empire across the North and South Americas. These are not simple daydreams but ideas that map out Jerrick's destiny. Jerrick rises out of the wreckage and devastation of the Michigan economy and turns his dreams into reality. Jerrick Davis and his political party, the National Workers' Party, took over the United States government and the rest of the Americas. Jerrick Ray Davis becomes the most powerful man in the 21st century, and the world trembles at his sight. Jerrick Ray Davis also makes a promise to the people. After the 2008 Financial Crisis, he will put all Americans back to work. Good-paying jobs will be plentiful again. Of course, Jerrick Davis puts everyone back to work, building his Empire. This story is about Jerrick Ray Davis' life from early childhood to rising in power. Please read this story with caution; we may be all toiling hard on Jerrick Ray Davis' Empire. As Jerrick Ray Davis says, "All Americans will be united under one flag."

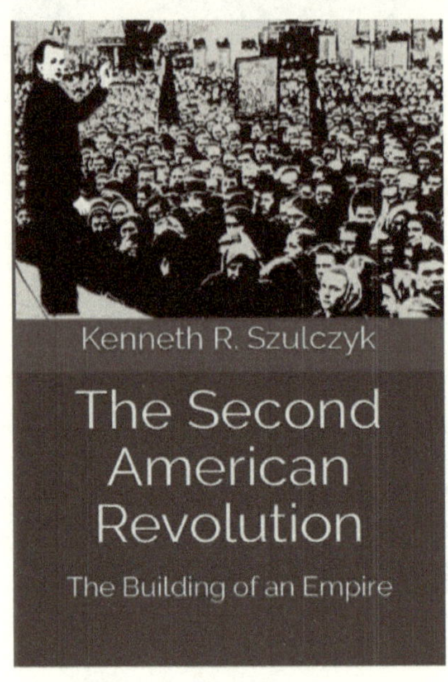
Kenneth R. Szulczyk
The Second
American
Revolution
The Building of an Empire

www.ingramcontent.com/pod-product-compliance
Lightning Source LLC
Chambersburg PA
CBHW031059250726
48655CB00004B/1507